DOVER · THRIFT · EDITIONS

The Rime of the Ancient Mariner and Other Poems

SAMUEL TAYLOR COLERIDGE

DOVER PUBLICATIONS, INC.
New York

DOVER THRIFT EDITIONS

EDITOR: STANLEY APPELBAUM

Published in Canada by General Publishing Company, Ltd., 30 Lesmill Road, Don Mills, Toronto, Ontario.
Published in the United Kingdom by Constable and Company, Ltd., 3 The Lanchesters, 162–164 Fulham Palace Road, London W6 9ER.

This new anthology, first published by Dover Publications, Inc., in 1992, contains 23 complete poems reprinted from *The Poems of Samuel Taylor Coleridge*, edited by Ernest Hartley Coleridge and published by Humphrey Milford / Oxford University Press, London, in 1917. The Note and the alphabetical lists of titles and first lines were prepared specially for the present edition.

Manufactured in the United States of America
Dover Publications, Inc., 31 East 2nd Street, Mineola, N.Y. 11501

Library of Congress Cataloging-in-Publication Data

Coleridge, Samuel Taylor, 1772–1834.
    The rime of the ancient mariner and other poems / Samuel Taylor Coleridge.
    p.   cm. — (Dover thrift editions)
  ISBN 0-486-27266-4 (pbk.)
  I. Title. II. Series.
PR4479.A1   1992a
821′.7—dc20
                                                                92-8111
                                                                 CIP

Note

SAMUEL TAYLOR COLERIDGE (1772–1834) was one of the principal English authors of the Romantic era. His works include not only poems, chiefly composed in his youth and early manhood, but also significant literary criticism and writings of religious, philosophical and social import. This new selection of 23 complete poems naturally includes the two that are considered among the greatest in the English language— "The Rime of the Ancient Mariner" and "Kubla Khan"—but also a number of his other most widely read and quoted pieces: reflective odes, the long narrative "Christabel" and a few short but pungent epigrams. The poems are arranged in chronological order by date of composition (see the table of contents for details; some scholars accept Coleridge's own dating of 1797 for "Kubla Khan").

Three of the works—"The Dungeon," "The Rime of the Ancient Mariner" and "The Nightingale"—formed part of *Lyrical Ballads,* the epoch-making volume Coleridge published in conjunction with his friend Wordsworth in 1798. A number of poems reflect Coleridge's trip to Germany in 1798 and his ongoing interest in the progressive German writing of the time: the sonnet to Schiller, "Christabel" (strongly influenced by such works as Gottfried August Bürger's ballad "Lenore" of 1773), "Something Childish" (a close adaptation of the well-known folksong "Wenn ich ein Vöglein wär' ") and the elegiac couplet on Ovidian meter, reminiscent of famous epigrams by Schiller and Goethe. The Ovidian piece also recalls Coleridge's role as literary historian and critic, as do the poems concerning Schiller and Donne. "France: An Ode" represents one aspect of his political thought. A few of the poems exemplify his wit, particularly "Cologne" and "On a Ruined House in a Romantic Country," in which the poet parodied his own manner and that of his close friends Charles Lamb and Charles Lloyd (the latter of whom was probably the Charles addressed in the "Sonnet: To a Friend Who Asked . . .").

Contents

The dates in brackets are those of composition.

To the Author of 'The Robbers'

Schiller! that hour I would have wish'd to die
If thro' the shuddering midnight I had sent
From the dark dungeon of the Tower time-rent
That fearful voice, a famish'd Father's cry—
Lest in some after moment aught more mean
Might stamp me mortal! A triumphant shout
Black Horror scream'd, and all her *goblin* rout
Diminish'd shrunk from the more withering scene!
Ah! Bard tremendous in sublimity!
Could I behold thee in thy loftier mood
Wandering at eve with finely-frenzied eye
Beneath some wast old tempest-swinging wood!
Awhile with mute awe gazing I would brood:
Then weep aloud in a wild ecstasy!

Sonnet

TO A FRIEND WHO ASKED, HOW I FELT WHEN THE NURSE
FIRST PRESENTED MY INFANT TO ME

Charles! my slow heart was only sad, when first
   I scann'd that face of feeble infancy:
For dimly on my thoughtful spirit burst
   All I had been, and all my child might be!
But when I saw it on its mother's arm,
   And hanging at her bosom (she the while
   Bent o'er its features with a tearful smile)
Then I was thrill'd and melted, and most warm
Impress'd a father's kiss: and all beguil'd
   Of dark remembrance and presageful fear,
   I seem'd to see an angel-form appear—
'Twas even thine, belovéd woman mild!
   So for the mother's sake the child was dear,
And dearer was the mother for the child.

1

This Lime-Tree Bower My Prison

Well, they are gone, and here must I remain,
This lime-tree bower my prison! I have lost
Beauties and feelings, such as would have been
Most sweet to my remembrance even when age
Had dimm'd mine eyes to blindness! They, meanwhile,
Friends, whom I never more may meet again,
On springy heath, along the hill-top edge,
Wander in gladness, and wind down, perchance,
To that still roaring dell, of which I told;
The roaring dell, o'erwooded, narrow, deep,
And only speckled by the mid-day sun;
Where its slim trunk the ash from rock to rock
Flings arching like a bridge;—that branchless ash,
Unsunn'd and damp, whose few poor yellow leaves
Ne'er tremble in the gale, yet tremble still,
Fann'd by the water-fall! and there my friends
Behold the dark green file of long lank weeds,
That all at once (a most fantastic sight!)
Still nod and drip beneath the dripping edge
Of the blue clay-stone.

          Now, my friends emerge
Beneath the wide wide Heaven—and view again
The many-steepled tract magnificent
Of hilly fields and meadows, and the sea,
With some fair bark, perhaps, whose sails light up
The slip of smooth clear blue betwixt two Isles
Of purple shadow! Yes! they wander on
In gladness all; but thou, methinks, most glad,
My gentle-hearted Charles! for thou hast pined
And hunger'd after Nature, many a year,
In the great City pent, winning thy way
With sad yet patient soul, through evil and pain
And strange calamity! Ah! slowly sink
Behind the western ridge, thou glorious Sun!
Shine in the slant beams of the sinking orb,
Ye purple heath-flowers! richlier burn, ye clouds!
Live in the yellow light, ye distant groves!
And kindle, thou blue Ocean! So my friend

Struck with deep joy may stand, as I have stood,
Silent with swimming sense; yea, gazing round
On the wide landscape, gaze till all doth seem
Less gross than bodily; and of such hues
As veil the Almighty Spirit, when yet he makes
Spirits perceive his presence.

                      A delight
Comes sudden on my heart, and I am glad
As I myself were there! Nor in this bower,
This little lime-tree bower, have I not mark'd
Much that has sooth'd me. Pale beneath the blaze
Hung the transparent foliage; and I watch'd
Some broad and sunny leaf, and lov'd to see
The shadow of the leaf and stem above
Dappling its sunshine! And that walnut-tree
Was richly ting'd, and a deep radiance lay
Full on the ancient ivy, which usurps
Those fronting elms, and now, with blackest mass
Makes their dark branches gleam a lighter hue
Through the late twilight: and though now the bat
Wheels silent by, and not a swallow twitters,
Yet still the solitary humble-bee
Sings in the bean-flower! Henceforth I shall know
That Nature ne'er deserts the wise and pure;
No plot so narrow, be but Nature there,
No waste so vacant, but may well employ
Each faculty of sense, and keep the heart
Awake to Love and Beauty! and sometimes
'Tis well to be bereft of promis'd good,
That we may lift the soul, and contemplate
With lively joy the joys we cannot share.
My gentle-hearted Charles! when the last rook
Beat its straight path along the dusky air
Homewards, I blest it! deeming its black wing
(Now a dim speck, now vanishing in light)
Had cross'd the mighty Orb's dilated glory,
While thou stood'st gazing; or, when all was still,
Flew creeking o'er thy head, and had a charm
For thee, my gentle-hearted Charles, to whom
No sound is dissonant which tells of Life.

The Dungeon

And this place our forefathers made for man!
This is the process of our love and wisdom,
To each poor brother who offends against us—
Most innocent, perhaps—and what if guilty?
Is this the only cure? Merciful God!
Each pore and natural outlet shrivell'd up
By Ignorance and parching Poverty,
His energies roll back upon his heart,
And stagnate and corrupt; till chang'd to poison,
They break out on him, like a loathsome plague-spot;
Then we call in our pamper'd mountebanks—
And this is their best cure! uncomforted
And friendless solitude, groaning and tears,
And savage faces, at the clanking hour,
Seen through the steams and vapour of his dungeon,
By the lamp's dismal twilight! So he lies
Circled with evil, till his very soul
Unmoulds its essence, hopelessly deform'd
By sights of ever more deformity!

With other ministrations thou, O Nature!
Healest thy wandering and distemper'd child:
Thou pourest on him thy soft influences,
Thy sunny hues, fair forms, and breathing sweets,
Thy melodies of woods, and winds, and waters,
Till he relent, and can no more endure
To be a jarring and a dissonant thing,
Amid this general dance and minstrelsy;
But, bursting into tears, wins back his way,
His angry spirit heal'd and harmoniz'd
By the benignant touch of Love and Beauty.

The Rime of the Ancient Mariner

IN SEVEN PARTS

Facile credo, plures esse Naturas invisibiles quam visibiles in rerum universitate. Sed horum omnium familiam quis nobis enarrabit? et gradus et cognationes et discrimina et singulorum munera? Quid agunt? quae loca habitant? Harum rerum notitiam semper ambivit ingenium humanum, nunquam attigit. Juvat, interea, non diffiteor, quandoque in animo, tanquam in tabula, majoris et melioris mundi imaginem contemplari: ne mens assuefacta hodiernae vitae minutiis se contrahat nimis, et tota subsidat in pusillas cogitationes. Sed veritati interea invigilandum est, modusque servandus, ut certa ab incertis, diem a nocte, distinguamus.—T. BURNET, *Archaeol. Phil.* p. 68.*

ARGUMENT

How a Ship having passed the Line was driven by storms to the cold Country towards the South Pole; and how from thence she made her course to the tropical Latitude of the Great Pacific Ocean; and of the strange things that befell; and in what manner the Ancyent Marinere came back to his own Country.

Part I

An ancient Mariner meeteth three Gallants bidden to a wedding-feast, and detaineth one.

It is an ancient Mariner,
And he stoppeth one of three.
'By thy long grey beard and glittering eye,
Now wherefore stopp'st thou me?

The Bridegroom's doors are opened wide,
And I am next of kin;
The guests are met, the feast is set:
May'st hear the merry din.'

---

* TRANSLATION: I readily believe that in the totality of things there are more invisible than visible natures. But who shall recount to us the family of all these things? and their degrees and relationships and distinctive signs and their individual functions? What do they do? What places do they inhabit? The human mind has always solicited knowledge of these matters but has never attained it. Meanwhile, I do not deny, it is sometimes pleasant to contemplate the image of a greater and better world in the mind as if in a picture, lest the mind, accustomed to the trivia of modern life, should shrink excessively and sink completely into petty musings. But at the same time one must be intent upon truth, and moderation must be observed, so that we may distinguish the sure from the unsure, day from night.

He holds him with his skinny hand,
'There was a ship,' quoth he.
'Hold off! unhand me, grey-beard loon!'
Eftsoons his hand dropt he.

The Wedding-Guest is spellbound by the eye of the old seafaring man, and constrained to hear his tale.

He holds him with his glittering eye—
The Wedding-Guest stood still,
And listens like a three years' child:
The Mariner hath his will.

The Wedding-Guest sat on a stone:
He cannot choose but hear;
And thus spake on that ancient man,
The bright-eyed Mariner.

'The ship was cheered, the harbour cleared,
Merrily did we drop

The Mariner tells how the ship sailed southward with a good wind and fair weather, till it reached the line.

Below the kirk, below the hill,
Below the lighthouse top.

The Sun came up upon the left,
Out of the sea came he!
And he shone bright, and on the right
Went down into the sea.

Higher and higher every day,
Till over the mast at noon—'
The Wedding-Guest here beat his breast,
For he heard the loud bassoon.

The Wedding-Guest heareth the bridal music; but the Mariner continueth his tale.

The bride hath paced into the hall,
Red as a rose is she;
Nodding their heads before her goes
The merry minstrelsy.

The Wedding-Guest he beat his breast,
Yet he cannot choose but hear;
And thus spake on that ancient man,
The bright-eyed Mariner.

The ship driven by a storm toward the south pole.

'And now the STORM-BLAST came, and he
Was tyrannous and strong:
He struck with his o'ertaking wings,
And chased us south along.

With sloping masts and dipping prow,
As who pursued with yell and blow
Still treads the shadow of his foe,
And forward bends his head,
The ship drove fast, loud roared the blast,
And southward aye we fled.

And now there came both mist and snow,
And it grew wondrous cold:
And ice, mast-high, came floating by,
As green as emerald.

The land of ice, and of fearful sounds where no living thing was to be seen.

And through the drifts the snowy clifts
Did send a dismal sheen:
Nor shapes of men nor beasts we ken—
The ice was all between.

The ice was here, the ice was there,
The ice was all around:
It cracked and growled, and roared and howled,
Like noises in a swound!

Till a great sea-bird, called the Albatross, came through the snow-fog, and was received with great joy and hospitality.

At length did cross an Albatross,
Thorough the fog it came;
As if it had been a Christian soul,
We hailed it in God's name.

It ate the food it ne'er had eat,
And round and round it flew.
The ice did split with a thunder-fit;
The helmsman steered us through!

And lo! the Albatross proveth a bird of good omen, and followeth the ship as it returned northward through fog and floating ice.

And a good south wind sprung up behind;
The Albatross did follow,
And every day, for food or play,
Came to the mariner's hollo!

In mist or cloud, on mast or shroud,
It perched for vespers nine;
Whiles all the night, through fog-smoke white,
Glimmered the white Moon-shine.'

The ancient Mariner inhospitably killeth the pious bird of good omen.

'God save thee, ancient Mariner!
From the fiends, that plague thee thus!—
Why look'st thou so?'—With my cross-bow
I shot the ALBATROSS.

Part II

The Sun now rose upon the right:
Out of the sea came he,
Still hid in mist, and on the left
Went down into the sea.

And the good south wind still blew behind,
But no sweet bird did follow,
Nor any day for food or play
Came to the mariners' hollo!

*His shipmates cry
out against the
ancient Mariner,
for killing the bird
of good luck.*

And I had done a hellish thing,
And it would work 'em woe:
For all averred, I had killed the bird
That made the breeze to blow.
Ah wretch! said they, the bird to slay,
That made the breeze to blow!

*But when the fog
cleared off, they
justify the same,
and thus make
themselves
accomplices in the
crime.*

Nor dim nor red, like God's own head,
The glorious Sun uprist:
Then all averred, I had killed the bird
That brought the fog and mist.
'Twas right, said they, such birds to slay,
That bring the fog and mist.

*The fair breeze
continues; the ship
enters the Pacific
Ocean, and sails
northward, even
till it reaches the
Line.*

The fair breeze blew, the white foam flew,
The furrow followed free;
We were the first that ever burst
Into that silent sea.

*The ship hath been
suddenly
becalmed.*

Down dropt the breeze, the sails dropt down,
'Twas sad as sad could be;
And we did speak only to break
The silence of the sea!

All in a hot and copper sky,
The bloody Sun, at noon,
Right up above the mast did stand,
No bigger than the Moon.

Day after day, day after day,
We stuck, nor breath nor motion;

As idle as a painted ship
Upon a painted ocean.

And the Albatross
begins to be
avenged.

Water, water, every where,
And all the boards did shrink;
Water, water, every where,
Nor any drop to drink.

The very deep did rot: O Christ!
That ever this should be!
Yea, slimy things did crawl with legs
Upon the slimy sea.

About, about, in reel and rout
The death-fires danced at night;
The water, like a witch's oils,
Burnt green, and blue and white.

A Spirit had
followed them; one
of the invisible
inhabitants of this
planet, neither

And some in dreams assuréd were
Of the Spirit that plagued us so;
Nine fathom deep he had followed us
From the land of mist and snow.

departed souls nor angels; concerning whom the learned Jew, Josephus, and the Platonic
Constantinopolitan, Michael Psellus, may be consulted. They are very numerous, and
there is no climate or element without one or more.

And every tongue, through utter drought,
Was withered at the root;
We could not speak, no more than if
We had been choked with soot.

The shipmates, in
their sore distress,
would fain throw
the whole guilt on
the ancient

Ah! well a-day! what evil looks
Had I from old and young!
Instead of the cross, the Albatross
About my neck was hung.

Mariner: in sign whereof they hang the dead sea-bird round his neck.

Part III

There passed a weary time. Each throat
Was parched, and glazed each eye.
A weary time! a weary time!
How glazed each weary eye,

*The ancient
Mariner beholdeth
a sign in the
element afar off.*

When looking westward, I beheld
A something in the sky.

At first it seemed a little speck,
And then it seemed a mist;
It moved and moved, and took at last
A certain shape, I wist.

A speck, a mist, a shape, I wist!
And still it neared and neared:
As if it dodged a water-sprite,
It plunged and tacked and veered.

*At its nearer
approach, it
seemeth him to be
a ship; and at a
dear ransom he
freeth his speech
from the bonds of
thirst.*

With throats unslaked, with black lips baked,
We could nor laugh nor wail;
Through utter drought all dumb we stood!
I bit my arm, I sucked the blood,
And cried, A sail! a sail!

A flash of joy;

With throats unslaked, with black lips baked,
Agape they heard me call:
Gramercy! they for joy did grin,
And all at once their breath drew in,
As they were drinking all.

*And horror follows.
For can it be a ship
that comes onward
without wind or
tide?*

See! see! (I cried) she tacks no more!
Hither to work us weal;
Without a breeze, without a tide,
She steadies with upright keel!

The western wave was all a-flame.
The day was well nigh done!
Almost upon the western wave
Rested the broad bright Sun;
When that strange shape drove suddenly
Betwixt us and the Sun.

*It seemeth him but
the skeleton of a
ship.*

And straight the Sun was flecked with bars,
(Heaven's Mother send us grace!)
As if through a dungeon-grate he peered
With broad and burning face.

*And its ribs are
seen as bars on the
face of the setting
Sun.*

Alas! (thought I, and my heart beat loud)
How fast she nears and nears!
Are those *her* sails that glance in the Sun,
Like restless gossameres?

The Spectre-
Woman and her
Deathmate, and
no other on board
the skeleton ship.

Are those *her* ribs through which the Sun
Did peer, as through a grate?
And is that Woman all her crew?
Is that a DEATH? and are there two?
Is DEATH that woman's mate?

Like vessel,
like crew!

Death and Life-
in-Death have
diced for the ship's
crew, and she (the
latter) winneth the
ancient Mariner.

Her lips were red, *her* looks were free,
Her locks were yellow as gold:
Her skin was as white as leprosy,
The Night-mare LIFE-IN-DEATH was she,
Who thicks man's blood with cold.

The naked hulk alongside came,
And the twain were casting dice;
'The game is done! I've won! I've won!'
Quoth she, and whistles thrice.

No twilight within
the courts of the
Sun.

The Sun's rim dips; the stars rush out:
At one stride comes the dark;
With far-heard whisper, o'er the sea,
Off shot the spectre-bark.

At the rising of the
Moon,

We listened and looked sideways up!
Fear at my heart, as at a cup,
My life-blood seemed to sip!
The stars were dim, and thick the night,
The steersman's face by his lamp gleamed white;
From the sails the dew did drip—
Till clomb above the eastern bar
The hornéd Moon, with one bright star
Within the nether tip.

One after another,

One after one, by the star-dogged Moon,
Too quick for groan or sigh,
Each turned his face with a ghastly pang,
And cursed me with his eye.

His shipmates drop
down dead.

Four times fifty living men,
(And I heard nor sigh nor groan)
With heavy thump, a lifeless lump,
They dropped down one by one.

But Life-in-Death
begins her work on
the ancient
Mariner.

The souls did from their bodies fly,—
They fled to bliss or woe!
And every soul, it passed me by,
Like the whizz of my cross-bow!

Part IV

*The Wedding-
Guest feareth that
a Spirit is talking
to him;*

'I fear thee, ancient Mariner!
I fear thy skinny hand!
And thou art long, and lank, and brown,
As is the ribbed sea-sand.

I fear thee and thy glittering eye,
And thy skinny hand, so brown.'—

*But the ancient
Mariner assureth
him of his bodily
life, and
proceedeth to relate
his horrible
penance.*

Fear not, fear not, thou Wedding-Guest!
This body dropt not down.

Alone, alone, all, all alone,
Alone on a wide wide sea!
And never a saint took pity on
My soul in agony.

*He despiseth the
creatures of the
calm,*

The many men, so beautiful!
And they all dead did lie:
And a thousand thousand slimy things
Lived on; and so did I.

*And envieth that
they should live,
and so many lie
dead.*

I looked upon the rotting sea,
And drew my eyes away;
I looked upon the rotting deck,
And there the dead men lay.

I looked to heaven, and tried to pray;
But or ever a prayer had gusht,
A wicked whisper came, and made
My heart as dry as dust.

I closed my lids, and kept them close,
And the balls like pulses beat;
For the sky and the sea, and the sea and the sky
Lay like a load on my weary eye,
And the dead were at my feet.

*But the curse liveth
for him in the eye
of the dead men.*

The cold sweat melted from their limbs,
Nor rot nor reek did they:
The look with which they looked on me
Had never passed away.

An orphan's curse would drag to hell
A spirit from on high;
But oh! more horrible than that

Is the curse in a dead man's eye!
Seven days, seven nights, I saw that curse,
And yet I could not die.

*In his loneliness
and fixedness he
yearneth towards
the journeying
Moon, and the
stars that still
sojourn, yet still
move onward; and
every where the
blue sky belongs to
them, and is their
appointed rest, and*

The moving Moon went up the sky,
And no where did abide:
Softly she was going up,
And a star or two beside—

Her beams bemocked the sultry main,
Like April hoar-frost spread;
But where the ship's huge shadow lay,
The charméd water burnt alway
A still and awful red.

*their native country and their own natural homes, which they enter unannounced, as
lords that are certainly expected and yet there is a silent joy at their arrival.*

*By the light of the
Moon he beholdeth
God's creatures of
the great calm.*

Beyond the shadow of the ship,
I watched the water-snakes:
They moved in tracks of shining white,
And when they reared, the elfish light
Fell off in hoary flakes.

Within the shadow of the ship
I watched their rich attire:
Blue, glossy green, and velvet black,
They coiled and swam; and every track
Was a flash of golden fire.

*Their beauty and
their happiness.*

O happy living things! no tongue
Their beauty might declare:
A spring of love gushed from my heart,

*He blesseth them
in his heart.*

And I blessed them unaware:
Sure my kind saint took pity on me,
And I blessed them unaware.

*The spell begins to
break.*

The self-same moment I could pray;
And from my neck so free
The Albatross fell off, and sank
Like lead into the sea.

Part V

Oh sleep! it is a gentle thing,
Beloved from pole to pole!

To Mary Queen the praise be given!
She sent the gentle sleep from Heaven,
That slid into my soul.

*By grace of the
holy Mother, the
ancient Mariner is
refreshed with rain.*

The silly buckets on the deck,
That had so long remained,
I dreamt that they were filled with dew;
And when I awoke, it rained.

My lips were wet, my throat was cold,
My garments all were dank;
Sure I had drunken in my dreams,
And still my body drank.

I moved, and could not feel my limbs:
I was so light—almost
I thought that I had died in sleep,
And was a blesséd ghost.

*He heareth sounds
and seeth strange
sights and
commotions in the
sky and the
element.*

And soon I heard a roaring wind:
It did not come anear;
But with its sound it shook the sails,
That were so thin and sere.

The upper air burst into life!
And a hundred fire-flags sheen,
To and fro they were hurried about!
And to and fro, and in and out,
The wan stars danced between.

And the coming wind did roar more loud,
And the sails did sigh like sedge;
And the rain poured down from one black cloud;
The Moon was at its edge.

The thick black cloud was cleft, and still
The Moon was at its side:
Like waters shot from some high crag,
The lightning fell with never a jag,
A river steep and wide.

*The bodies of the
ship's crew are
inspired and the
ship moves on;*

The loud wind never reached the ship,
Yet now the ship moved on!
Beneath the lightning and the Moon
The dead men gave a groan.

They groaned, they stirred, they all uprose,
Nor spake, nor moved their eyes;
It had been strange, even in a dream,
To have seen those dead men rise.

The helmsman steered, the ship moved on;
Yet never a breeze up-blew;
The mariners all 'gan work the ropes,
Where they were wont to do;
They raised their limbs like lifeless tools—
We were a ghastly crew.

The body of my brother's son
Stood by me, knee to knee:
The body and I pulled at one rope,
But he said nought to me.

'I fear thee, ancient Mariner!'
Be calm, thou Wedding-Guest!
'Twas not those souls that fled in pain,
Which to their corses came again,
But a troop of spirits blest:

But not by the souls of the men, nor by dæmons of earth or middle air, but by a blessed troop of angelic spirits, sent down by the invocation of the guardian saint.

For when it dawned—they dropped their arms,
And clustered round the mast;
Sweet sounds rose slowly through their mouths,
And from their bodies passed.

Around, around, flew each sweet sound,
Then darted to the Sun;
Slowly the sounds came back again,
Now mixed, now one by one.

Sometimes a-dropping from the sky
I heard the sky-lark sing;
Sometimes all little birds that are,
How they seemed to fill the sea and air
With their sweet jargoning!

And now 'twas like all instruments,
Now like a lonely flute;
And now it is an angel's song,
That makes the heavens be mute.

It ceased; yet still the sails made on
A pleasant noise till noon,
A noise like of a hidden brook
In the leafy month of June,
That to the sleeping woods all night
Singeth a quiet tune.

Till noon we quietly sailed on,
Yet never a breeze did breathe:
Slowly and smoothly went the ship,
Moved onward from beneath.

The lonesome Spirit from the south-pole carries on the ship as far as the Line, in obedience to the angelic troop, but still requireth vengeance.

Under the keel nine fathom deep,
From the land of mist and snow,
The spirit slid: and it was he
That made the ship to go.
The sails at noon left off their tune,
And the ship stood still also.

The Sun, right up above the mast,
Had fixed her to the ocean:
But in a minute she 'gan stir,
With a short uneasy motion—
Backwards and forwards half her length
With a short uneasy motion.

Then like a pawing horse let go,
She made a sudden bound:
It flung the blood into my head,
And I fell down in a swound.

The Polar Spirit's fellow-dæmons, the invisible inhabitants of the element, take part in his wrong; and two of them relate, one to the other, that penance long and heavy for the ancient Mariner hath been accorded to the Polar Spirit, who returneth southward.

How long in that same fit I lay,
I have not to declare;
But ere my living life returned,
I heard and in my soul discerned
Two voices in the air.

'Is it he?' quoth one, 'Is this the man?
By him who died on cross,
With his cruel bow he laid full low
The harmless Albatross.

The spirit who bideth by himself
In the land of mist and snow,
He loved the bird that loved the man
Who shot him with his bow.'

The other was a softer voice,
As soft as honey-dew:
Quoth he, 'The man hath penance done,
And penance more will do.'

Part VI

FIRST VOICE

'But tell me, tell me! speak again,
Thy soft response renewing—
What makes that ship drive on so fast?
What is the ocean doing?'

SECOND VOICE ·

'Still as a slave before his lord,
The ocean hath no blast;
His great bright eye most silently
Up to the Moon is cast—

If he may know which way to go;
For she guides him smooth or grim.
See, brother, see! how graciously
She looketh down on him.'

FIRST VOICE

The Mariner hath been cast into a trance; for the angelic power causeth the vessel to drive northward faster than human life could endure.

'But why drives on that ship so fast,
Without or wave or wind?'

SECOND VOICE

'The air is cut away before,
And closes from behind.

Fly, brother, fly! more high, more high!
Or we shall be belated:
For slow and slow that ship will go,
When the Mariner's trance is abated.'

The supernatural motion is retarded; the Mariner awakes, and his penance begins anew.

I woke, and we were sailing on
As in a gentle weather:
'Twas night, calm night, the moon was high;
The dead men stood together.

All stood together on the deck,
For a charnel-dungeon fitter:
All fixed on me their stony eyes,
That in the Moon did glitter.

The pang, the curse, with which they died,
Had never passed away:
I could not draw my eyes from theirs,
Nor turn them up to pray.

*The curse is finally
expiated.*

And now this spell was snapt: once more
I viewed the ocean green,
And looked far forth, yet little saw
Of what had else been seen—

Like one, that on a lonesome road
Doth walk in fear and dread,
And having once turned round walks on,
And turns no more his head;
Because he knows, a frightful fiend
Doth close behind him tread.

But soon there breathed a wind on me,
Nor sound nor motion made:
Its path was not upon the sea,
In ripple or in shade.

It raised my hair, it fanned my cheek
Like a meadow-gale of spring—
It mingled strangely with my fears,
Yet it felt like a welcoming.

Swiftly, swiftly flew the ship,
Yet she sailed softly too:
Sweetly, sweetly blew the breeze—
On me alone it blew.

*And the ancient
Mariner beholdeth
his native country.*

Oh! dream of joy! is this indeed
The light-house top I see?
Is this the hill? is this the kirk?
Is this mine own countree?

We drifted o'er the harbour-bar,
And I with sobs did pray—

O let me be awake, my God!
Or let me sleep alway.

The harbour-bay was clear as glass,
So smoothly it was strewn!
And on the bay the moonlight lay,
And the shadow of the Moon.

The rock shone bright, the kirk no less,
That stands above the rock:
The moonlight steeped in silentness
The steady weathercock.

And the bay was white with silent light,
Till rising from the same,
The angelic spirits Full many shapes, that shadows were,
leave the dead In crimson colours came.
bodies,

And appear in A little distance from the prow
their own forms of Those crimson shadows were:
light. I turned my eyes upon the deck—
Oh, Christ! what saw I there!

Each corse lay flat, lifeless and flat,
And, by the holy rood!
A man all light, a seraph-man,
On every corse there stood.

This seraph-band, each waved his hand:
It was a heavenly sight!
They stood as signals to the land,
Each one a lovely light;

This seraph-band, each waved his hand,
No voice did they impart—
No voice; but oh! the silence sank
Like music on my heart.

But soon I heard the dash of oars,
I heard the Pilot's cheer;
My head was turned perforce away
And I saw a boat appear.

The Pilot and the Pilot's boy,
I heard them coming fast:

Dear Lord in Heaven! it was a joy
The dead men could not blast.

I saw a third—I heard his voice:
It is the Hermit good!
He singeth loud his godly hymns
That he makes in the wood.
He'll shrieve my soul, he'll wash away
The Albatross's blood.

Part VII

*The Hermit of the
Wood,*

This Hermit good lives in that wood
Which slopes down to the sea.
How loudly his sweet voice he rears!
He loves to talk with marineres
That come from a far countree.

He kneels at morn, and noon, and eve—
He hath a cushion plump:
It is the moss that wholly hides
The rotted old oak-stump.

The skiff-boat neared: I heard them talk,
'Why, this is strange, I trow!
Where are those lights so many and fair,
That signal made but now?'

*Approacheth the
ship with wonder.*

'Strange, by my faith!' the Hermit said—
'And they answered not our cheer!
The planks looked warped! and see those sails,
How thin they are and sere!
I never saw aught like to them,
Unless perchance it were

Brown skeletons of leaves that lag
My forest-brook along;
When the ivy-tod is heavy with snow,
And the owlet whoops to the wolf below,
That eats the she-wolf's young.'

'Dear Lord! it hath a fiendish look—
(The Pilot made reply)
I am a-feared'—'Push on, push on!'
Said the Hermit cheerily.

The boat came closer to the ship,
But I nor spake nor stirred;
The boat came close beneath the ship,
And straight a sound was heard.

The ship suddenly
sinketh.

Under the water it rumbled on,
Still louder and more dread:
It reached the ship, it split the bay;
The ship went down like lead.

The ancient
Mariner is saved in
the Pilot's boat.

Stunned by that loud and dreadful sound,
Which sky and ocean smote,
Like one that hath been seven days drowned
My body lay afloat;
But swift as dreams, myself I found
Within the Pilot's boat.

Upon the whirl, where sank the ship,
The boat spun round and round;
And all was still, save that the hill
Was telling of the sound.

I moved my lips—the Pilot shrieked
And fell down in a fit;
The holy Hermit raised his eyes,
And prayed where he did sit.

I took the oars: the Pilot's boy,
Who now doth crazy go,
Laughed loud and long, and all the while
His eyes went to and fro.
'Ha! ha!' quoth he, 'full plain I see,
The Devil knows how to row.'

And now, all in my own countree,
I stood on the firm land!
The Hermit stepped forth from the boat,
And scarcely he could stand.

The ancient
Mariner earnestly
entreateth the
Hermit to shrieve
him; and the
penance of life falls
on him.

'O shrieve me, shrieve me, holy man!'
The Hermit crossed his brow.
'Say quick,' quoth he, 'I bid thee say—
What manner of man art thou?'

Forthwith this frame of mine was wrenched
With a woful agony,

Which forced me to begin my tale;
And then it left me free.

And ever and anon
throughout his
future life an
agony constraineth
him to travel from
land to land;

Since then, at an uncertain hour,
That agony returns:
And till my ghastly tale is told,
This heart within me burns.

I pass, like night, from land to land;
I have strange power of speech;
That moment that his face I see,
I know the man that must hear me:
To him my tale I teach.

What loud uproar bursts from that door!
The wedding-guests are there:
But in the garden-bower the bride
And bride-maids singing are:
And hark the little vesper bell,
Which biddeth me to prayer!

O Wedding-Guest! this soul hath been
Alone on a wide wide sea:
So lonely 'twas, that God himself
Scarce seeméd there to be.

O sweeter than the marriage-feast,
'Tis sweeter far to me,
To walk together to the kirk
With a goodly company!—

To walk together to the kirk,
And all together pray,
While each to his great Father bends,
Old men, and babes, and loving friends
And youths and maidens gay!

And to teach, by
his own example,
love and reverence
to all things that
God made and
loveth.

Farewell, farewell! but this I tell
To thee, thou Wedding-Guest!
He prayeth well, who loveth well
Both man and bird and beast.

He prayeth best, who loveth best
All things both great and small;

For the dear God who loveth us,
He made and loveth all.

The Mariner, whose eye is bright,
Whose beard with age is hoar,
Is gone: and now the Wedding-Guest
Turned from the bridegroom's door.

He went like one that hath been stunned,
And is of sense forlorn:
A sadder and a wiser man,
He rose the morrow morn.

On a Ruined House in a Romantic Country

And this reft house is that the which he built,
Lamented Jack! And here his malt he pil'd,
Cautious in vain! These rats that squeak so wild,
Squeak, not unconscious of their father's guilt.
Did ye not see her gleaming thro' the glade?
Belike, 'twas she, the maiden all forlorn.
What though she milk no cow with crumpled horn,
Yet *aye* she haunts the dale where *erst* she stray'd;
And *aye* beside her stalks her amorous knight!
Still on his thighs their wonted brogues are worn,
And thro' those brogues, still tatter'd and betorn,
His hindward charms gleam an unearthly white;
As when thro' broken clouds at night's high noon
Peeps in fair fragments forth the full-orb'd harvest-moon!

Christabel

Part I

'Tis the middle of night by the castle clock,
And the owls have awakened the crowing cock;
Tu—whit!—Tu—whoo!
And hark, again! the crowing cock,
How drowsily it crew.

Sir Leoline, the Baron rich,
Hath a toothless mastiff bitch;
From her kennel beneath the rock
She maketh answer to the clock,
Four for the quarters, and twelve for the hour;
Ever and aye, by shine and shower,
Sixteen short howls, not over loud;
Some say, she sees my lady's shroud.

Is the night chilly and dark?
The night is chilly, but not dark,
The thin gray cloud is spread on high,
It covers but not hides the sky.
The moon is behind, and at the full;
And yet she looks both small and dull.
The night is chill, the cloud is gray:
'Tis a month before the month of May,
And the Spring comes slowly up this way.

The lovely lady, Christabel,
Whom her father loves so well,
What makes her in the wood so late,
A furlong from the castle gate?
She had dreams all yesternight
Of her own betrothéd knight;
And she in the midnight wood will pray
For the weal of her lover that's far away.

She stole along, she nothing spoke,
The sighs she heaved were soft and low,
And naught was green upon the oak

But moss and rarest misletoe:
She kneels beneath the huge oak tree,
And in silence prayeth she.

The lady sprang up suddenly,
The lovely lady, Christabel!
It moaned as near, as near can be,
But what it is she cannot tell.—
On the other side it seems to be,
Of the huge, broad-breasted, old oak tree.

The night is chill; the forest bare;
Is it the wind that moaneth bleak?
There is not wind enough in the air
To move away the ringlet curl
From the lovely lady's cheek—
There is not wind enough to twirl
The one red leaf, the last of its clan,
That dances as often as dance it can,
Hanging so light, and hanging so high,
On the topmost twig that looks up at the sky.

Hush, beating heart of Christabel!
Jesu, Maria, shield her well!
She folded her arms beneath her cloak,
And stole to the other side of the oak.
        What sees she there?

There she sees a damsel bright,
Drest in a silken robe of white,
That shadowy in the moonlight shone:
The neck that made that white robe wan,
Her stately neck, and arms were bare;
Her blue-veined feet unsandal'd were,
And wildly glittered here and there
The gems entangled in her hair.

I guess, 'twas frightful there to see
A lady so richly clad as she—
Beautiful exceedingly!

Mary mother, save me now!
(Said Christabel,) And who art thou?

The lady strange made answer meet,
And her voice was faint and sweet:—
Have pity on my sore distress,
I scarce can speak for weariness:
Stretch forth thy hand, and have no fear!
Said Christabel, How camest thou here?
And the lady, whose voice was faint and sweet,
Did thus pursue her answer meet:—

My sire is of a noble line,
And my name is Geraldine:
Five warriors seized me yestermorn,
Me, even me, a maid forlorn:
They choked my cries with force and fright,
And tied me on a palfrey white.
The palfrey was as fleet as wind,
And they rode furiously behind.
They spurred amain, their steeds were white:
And once we crossed the shade of night.
As sure as Heaven shall rescue me,
I have no thought what men they be;
Nor do I know how long it is
(For I have lain entranced I wis)
Since one, the tallest of the five,
Took me from the palfrey's back,
A weary woman, scarce alive.
Some muttered words his comrades spoke:
He placed me underneath this oak;
He swore they would return with haste;
Whither they went I cannot tell—
I thought I heard, some minutes past,
Sounds as of a castle bell.
Stretch forth thy hand (thus ended she),
And help a wretched maid to flee.

Then Christabel stretched forth her hand,
And comforted fair Geraldine:
O well, bright dame! may you command
The service of Sir Leoline;
And gladly our stout chivalry
Will he send forth and friends withal

To guide and guard you safe and free
Home to your noble father's hall.

She rose: and forth with steps they passed
That strove to be, and were not, fast.
Her gracious stars the lady blest,
And thus spake on sweet Christabel:
All our household are at rest,
The hall as silent as the cell;
Sir Leoline is weak in health,
And may not well awakened be,
But we will move as if in stealth,
And I beseech your courtesy,
This night, to share your couch with me.

They crossed the moat, and Christabel
Took the key that fitted well;
A little door she opened straight,
All in the middle of the gate;
The gate that was ironed within and without,
Where an army in battle array had marched out.
The lady sank, belike through pain,
And Christabel with might and main
Lifted her up, a weary weight,
Over the threshold of the gate:
Then the lady rose again,
And moved, as she were not in pain.

So free from danger, free from fear,
They crossed the court: right glad they were.
And Christabel devoutly cried
To the lady by her side,
Praise we the Virgin all divine
Who hath rescued thee from thy distress!
Alas, alas! said Geraldine,
I cannot speak for weariness.
So free from danger, free from fear,
They crossed the court: right glad they were.

Outside her kennel, the mastiff old
Lay fast asleep, in moonshine cold.
The mastiff old did not awake,
Yet she an angry moan did make!

And what can ail the mastiff bitch?
Never till now she uttered yell
Beneath the eye of Christabel.
Perhaps it is the owlet's scritch:
For what can ail the mastiff bitch?

They passed the hall, that echoes still,
Pass as lightly as you will!
The brands were flat, the brands were dying,
Amid their own white ashes lying;
But when the lady passed, there came
A tongue of light, a fit of flame;
And Christabel saw the lady's eye,
And nothing else saw she thereby,
Save the boss of the shield of Sir Leoline tall,
Which hung in a murky old niche in the wall.
O softly tread, said Christabel,
My father seldom sleepeth well.

Sweet Christabel her feet doth bare,
And jealous of the listening air
They steal their way from stair to stair,
Now in glimmer, and now in gloom,
And now they pass the Baron's room,
As still as death, with stifled breath!
And now have reached her chamber door;
And now doth Geraldine press down
The rushes of the chamber floor.

The moon shines dim in the open air,
And not a moonbeam enters here.
But they without its light can see
The chamber carved so curiously,
Carved with figures strange and sweet,
All made out of the carver's brain,
For a lady's chamber meet:
The lamp with twofold silver chain
Is fastened to an angel's feet.

The silver lamp burns dead and dim;
But Christabel the lamp will trim.
She trimmed the lamp, and made it bright,
And left it swinging to and fro,

While Geraldine, in wretched plight,
Sank down upon the floor below.

O weary lady, Geraldine,
I pray you, drink this cordial wine!
It is a wine of virtuous powers;
My mother made it of wild flowers.

And will your mother pity me,
Who am a maiden most forlorn?
Christabel answered—Woe is me!
She died the hour that I was born.
I have heard the grey-haired friar tell
How on her death-bed she did say,
That she should hear the castle-bell
Strike twelve upon my wedding-day.
O mother dear! that thou wert here!
I would, said Geraldine, she were!
But soon with altered voice, said she—
'Off, wandering mother! Peak and pine!
I have power to bid thee flee.'
Alas! what ails poor Geraldine?
Why stares she with unsettled eye?
Can she the bodiless dead espy?
And why with hollow voice cries she,
'Off, woman, off! this hour is mine—
Though thou her guardian spirit be,
Off, woman, off! 'tis given to me.'

Then Christabel knelt by the lady's side,
And raised to heaven her eyes so blue—
Alas! said she, this ghastly ride—
Dear lady! it hath wildered you!
The lady wiped her moist cold brow,
And faintly said, ' 'tis over now!'

Again the wild-flower wine she drank:
Her fair large eyes 'gan glitter bright,
And from the floor whereon she sank,
The lofty lady stood upright:
She was most beautiful to see,
Like a lady of a far countrée.

And thus the lofty lady spake—
'All they who live in the upper sky,
Do love you, holy Christabel!
And you love them, and for their sake
And for the good which me befel,
Even I in my degree will try,
Fair maiden, to requite you well.
But now unrobe yourself; for I
Must pray, ere yet in bed I lie.'

Quoth Christabel, So let it be!
And as the lady bade, did she.
Her gentle limbs did she undress,
And lay down in her loveliness.

But through her brain of weal and woe
So many thoughts moved to and fro,
That vain it were her lids to close;
So half-way from the bed she rose,
And on her elbow did recline
To look at the lady Geraldine.

Beneath the lamp the lady bowed,
And slowly rolled her eyes around;
Then drawing in her breath aloud,
Like one that shuddered, she unbound
The cincture from beneath her breast:
Her silken robe, and inner vest,
Dropt to her feet, and full in view,
Behold! her bosom and half her side——
A sight to dream of, not to tell!
O shield her! shield sweet Christabel!

Yet Geraldine nor speaks nor stirs;
Ah! what a stricken look was hers!
Deep from within she seems half-way
To lift some weight with sick assay,
And eyes the maid and seeks delay;
Then suddenly, as one defied,
Collects herself in scorn and pride,
And lay down by the Maiden's side!—
And in her arms the maid she took,
                    Ah wel-a-day!

And with low voice and doleful look
These words did say:
'In the touch of this bosom there worketh a spell,
Which is lord of thy utterance, Christabel!
Thou knowest to-night, and wilt know to-morrow,
This mark of my shame, this seal of my sorrow;
      But vainly thou warrest,
        For this is alone in
      Thy power to declare,
        That in the dim forest
      Thou heard'st a low moaning,
And found'st a bright lady, surpassingly fair;
And didst bring her home with thee in love and in
    charity,
To shield her and shelter her from the damp air.'

THE CONCLUSION TO PART I

It was a lovely sight to see
The lady Christabel, when she
Was praying at the old oak tree.
      Amid the jaggéd shadows
      Of mossy leafless boughs,
      Kneeling in the moonlight,
      To make her gentle vows;
Her slender palms together prest,
Heaving sometimes on her breast;
Her face resigned to bliss or bale—
Her face, oh call it fair not pale,
And both blue eyes more bright than clear,
Each about to have a tear.

With open eyes (ah woe is me!)
Asleep, and dreaming fearfully,
Fearfully dreaming, yet, I wis,
Dreaming that alone, which is—
O sorrow and shame! Can this be she,
The lady, who knelt at the old oak tree?
And lo! the worker of these harms,
That holds the maiden in her arms,
Seems to slumber still and mild,
As a mother with her child.

A star hath set, a star hath risen,
O Geraldine! since arms of thine
Have been the lovely lady's prison.
O Geraldine! one hour was thine—
Thou'st had thy will! By tairn and rill,
The night-birds all that hour were still.
But now they are jubilant anew,
From cliff and tower, tu—whoo! tu—whoo!
Tu—whoo! tu—whoo! from wood and fell!

And see! the lady Christabel
Gathers herself from out her trance;
Her limbs relax, her countenance
Grows sad and soft; the smooth thin lids
Close o'er her eyes; and tears she sheds—
Large tears that leave the lashes bright!
And oft the while she seems to smile
As infants at a sudden light!

Yea, she doth smile, and she doth weep,
Like a youthful hermitess,
Beauteous in a wilderness,
Who, praying always, prays in sleep.
And, if she move unquietly,
Perchance, 'tis but the blood so free
Comes back and tingles in her feet.
No doubt, she hath a vision sweet.
What if her guardian spirit 'twere,
What if she knew her mother near?
But this she knows, in joys and woes,
That saints will aid if men will call:
For the blue sky bends over all!

Part II

Each matin bell, the Baron saith,
Knells us back to a world of death.
These words Sir Leoline first said,
When he rose and found his lady dead:
These words Sir Leoline will say
Many a morn to his dying day!

And hence the custom and law began
That still at dawn the sacristan,
Who duly pulls the heavy bell,
Five and forty beads must tell
Between each stroke—a warning knell,
Which not a soul can choose but hear
From Bratha Head to Wyndermere.

Saith Bracy the bard, So let it knell!
And let the drowsy sacristan
Still count as slowly as he can!
There is no lack of such, I ween,
As well fill up the space between.
In Langdale Pike and Witch's Lair,
And Dungeon-ghyll so foully rent,
With ropes of rock and bells of air
Three sinful sextons' ghosts are pent,
Who all give back, one after t'other,
The death-note to their living brother;
And oft too, by the knell offended,
Just as their one! two! three! is ended,
The devil mocks the doleful tale
With a merry peal from Borodale.

The air is still! through mist and cloud
That merry peal comes ringing loud;
And Geraldine shakes off her dread,
And rises lightly from the bed;
Puts on her silken vestments white,
And tricks her hair in lovely plight,
And nothing doubting of her spell
Awakens the lady Christabel.
'Sleep you, sweet lady Christabel?
I trust that you have rested well.'

And Christabel awoke and spied
The same who lay down by her side—
O rather say, the same whom she
Raised up beneath the old oak tree!
Nay, fairer yet! and yet more fair!
For she belike hath drunken deep
Of all the blessedness of sleep!

And while she spake, her looks, her air
Such gentle thankfulness declare,
That (so it seemed) her girded vests
Grew tight beneath her heaving breasts.
'Sure I have sinn'd!' said Christabel,
'Now heaven be praised if all be well!'
And in low faltering tones, yet sweet,
Did she the lofty lady greet
With such perplexity of mind
As dreams too lively leave behind.

So quickly she rose, and quickly arrayed
Her maiden limbs, and having prayed
That He, who on the cross did groan,
Might wash away her sins unknown,
She forthwith led fair Geraldine
To meet her sire, Sir Leoline.

The lovely maid and the lady tall
Are pacing both into the hall,
And pacing on through page and groom,
Enter the Baron's presence-room.

The Baron rose, and while he prest
His gentle daughter to his breast,
With cheerful wonder in his eyes
The lady Geraldine espies,
And gave such welcome to the same,
As might beseem so bright a dame!

But when he heard the lady's tale,
And when she told her father's name,
Why waxed Sir Leoline so pale,
Murmuring o'er the name again,
Lord Roland de Vaux of Tryermaine?

Alas! they had been friends in youth;
But whispering tongues can poison truth;
And constancy lives in realms above;
And life is thorny; and youth is vain;
And to be wroth with one we love
Doth work like madness in the brain.
And thus it chanced, as I divine,

With Roland and Sir Leoline.
Each spake words of high disdain
And insult to his heart's best brother:
They parted—ne'er to meet again!
But never either found another
To free the hollow heart from paining—
They stood aloof, the scars remaining,
Like cliffs which had been rent asunder;
A dreary sea now flows between;—
But neither heat, nor frost, nor thunder,
Shall wholly do away, I ween,
The marks of that which once hath been.

Sir Leoline, a moment's space,
Stood gazing on the damsel's face:
And the youthful Lord of Tryermaine
Came back upon his heart again.

O then the Baron forgot his age,
His noble heart swelled high with rage;
He swore by the wounds in Jesu's side
He would proclaim it far and wide,
With trump and solemn heraldry,
That they, who thus had wronged the dame,
Were base as spotted infamy!
'And if they dare deny the same,
My herald shall appoint a week,
And let the recreant traitors seek
My tourney court—that there and then
I may dislodge their reptile souls
From the bodies and forms of men!'
He spake: his eye in lightning rolls!
For the lady was ruthlessly seized; and he kenned
In the beautiful lady the child of his friend!

And now the tears were on his face,
And fondly in his arms he took
Fair Geraldine, who met the embrace,
Prolonging it with joyous look.
Which when she viewed, a vision fell
Upon the soul of Christabel,
The vision of fear, the touch and pain!.

She shrunk and shuddered, and saw again—
(Ah, woe is me! Was it for thee,
Thou gentle maid! such sights to see?)

Again she saw that bosom old,
Again she felt that bosom cold,
And drew in her breath with a hissing sound:
Whereat the Knight turned wildly round,
And nothing saw, but his own sweet maid
With eyes upraised, as one that prayed.

The touch, the sight, had passed away,
And in its stead that vision blest,
Which comforted her after-rest
While in the lady's arms she lay,
Had put a rapture in her breast,
And on her lips and o'er her eyes
Spread smiles like light!
                                    With new surprise,
'What ails then my belovéd child?'
The Baron said—His daughter mild
Made answer, 'All will yet be well!'
I ween, she had no power to tell
Aught else: so mighty was the spell.

Yet he, who saw this Geraldine,
Had deemed her sure a thing divine:
Such sorrow with such grace she blended,
As if she feared she had offended
Sweet Christabel, that gentle maid!
And with such lowly tones she prayed
She might be sent without delay
Home to her father's mansion.
                                              'Nay!
Nay, by my soul!' said Leoline.
'Ho! Bracy the bard, the charge be thine!
Go thou, with music sweet and loud,
And take two steeds with trappings proud,
And take the youth whom thou lov'st best
To bear thy harp, and learn thy song,
And clothe you both in solemn vest,
And over the mountains haste along,

Lest wandering folk, that are abroad,
Detain you on the valley road.

'And when he has crossed the Irthing flood,
My merry bard! he hastes, he hastes
Up Knorren Moor, through Halegarth Wood,
And reaches soon that castle good
Which stands and threatens Scotland's wastes.

'Bard Bracy! bard Bracy! your horses are fleet,
Ye must ride up the hall, your music so sweet,
More loud than your horses' echoing feet!
And loud and loud to Lord Roland call,
Thy daughter is safe in Langdale hall!
Thy beautiful daughter is safe and free—
Sir Leoline greets thee thus through me!
He bids thee come without delay
With all thy numerous array
And take thy lovely daughter home:
And he will meet thee on the way
With all his numerous array
White with their panting palfreys' foam:
And, by mine honour! I will say,
That I repent me of the day
When I spake words of fierce disdain
To Roland de Vaux of Tryermaine!—
—For since that evil hour hath flown,
Many a summer's sun hath shone;
Yet ne'er found I a friend again
Like Roland de Vaux of Tryermaine.'

The lady fell, and clasped his knees,
Her face upraised, her eyes o'erflowing;
And Bracy replied, with faltering voice,
His gracious Hail on all bestowing!—
'Thy words, thou sire of Christabel,
Are sweeter than my harp can tell;
Yet might I gain a boon of thee,
This day my journey should not be,
So strange a dream hath come to me,
That I had vowed with music loud
To clear yon wood from thing unblest,

Warned by a vision in my rest!
For in my sleep I saw that dove,
That gentle bird, whom thou dost love,
And call'st by thy own daughter's name—
Sir Leoline! I saw the same
Fluttering, and uttering fearful moan,
Among the green herbs in the forest alone.
Which when I saw and when I heard,
I wonder'd what might ail the bird;
For nothing near it could I see,
Save the grass and green herbs underneath the old tree.

'And in my dream methought I went
To search out what might there be found;
And what the sweet bird's trouble meant,
That thus lay fluttering on the ground.
I went and peered, and could descry
No cause for her distressful cry;
But yet for her dear lady's sake
I stooped, methought, the dove to take,
When lo! I saw a bright green snake
Coiled around its wings and neck.
Green as the herbs on which it couched,
Close by the dove's its head it crouched;
And with the dove it heaves and stirs,
Swelling its neck as she swelled hers!
I woke; it was the midnight hour,
The clock was echoing in the tower;
But though my slumber was gone by,
This dream it would not pass away—
It seems to live upon my eye!
And thence I vowed this self-same day
With music strong and saintly song
To wander through the forest bare,
Lest aught unholy loiter there.'

Thus Bracy said: the Baron, the while,
Half-listening heard him with a smile;
Then turned to Lady Geraldine,
His eyes made up of wonder and love;
And said in courtly accents fine,
'Sweet maid, Lord Roland's beauteous dove,

With arms more strong than harp or song,
Thy sire and I will crush the snake!'
He kissed her forehead as he spake,
And Geraldine in maiden wise
Casting down her large bright eyes,
With blushing cheek and courtesy fine
She turned her from Sir Leoline;
Softly gathering up her train,
That o'er her right arm fell again;
And folded her arms across her chest,
And couched her head upon her breast,
And looked askance at Christabel——
Jesu, Maria, shield her well!

A snake's small eye blinks dull and shy;
And the lady's eyes they shrunk in her head,
Each shrunk up to a serpent's eye,
And with somewhat of malice, and more of dread,
At Christabel she looked askance!—
One moment—and the sight was fled!
But Christabel in dizzy trance
Stumbling on the unsteady ground
Shuddered aloud, with a hissing sound;
And Geraldine again turned round,
And like a thing, that sought relief,
Full of wonder and full of grief,
She rolled her large bright eyes divine
Wildly on Sir Leoline.

The maid, alas! her thoughts are gone,
She nothing sees—no sight but one!
The maid, devoid of guile and sin,
I know not how, in fearful wise,
So deeply had she drunken in
That look, those shrunken serpent eyes,
That all her features were resigned
To this sole image in her mind:
And passively did imitate
That look of dull and treacherous hate!
And thus she stood, in dizzy trance,
Still picturing that look askance
With forced unconscious sympathy

Full before her father's view——
As far as such a look could be
In eyes so innocent and blue!

And when the trance was o'er, the maid
Paused awhile, and inly prayed:
Then falling at the Baron's feet,
'By my mother's soul do I entreat
That thou this woman send away!'
She said: and more she could not say:
For what she knew she could not tell,
O'er-mastered by the mighty spell.

Why is thy cheek so wan and wild,
Sir Leoline? Thy only child
Lies at thy feet, thy joy, thy pride,
So fair, so innocent, so mild;
The same, for whom thy lady died!
O by the pangs of her dear mother
Think thou no evil of thy child!
For her, and thee, and for no other,
She prayed the moment ere she died:
Prayed that the babe for whom she died,
Might prove her dear lord's joy and pride!
    That prayer her deadly pangs beguiled,
        Sir Leoline!
    And wouldst thou wrong thy only child,
        Her child and thine?

Within the Baron's heart and brain
If thoughts, like these, had any share,
They only swelled his rage and pain,
And did but work confusion there.
His heart was cleft with pain and rage,
His cheeks they quivered, his eyes were wild,
Dishonoured thus in his old age;
Dishonoured by his only child,
And all his hospitality
To the wronged daughter of his friend
By more than woman's jealousy
Brought thus to a disgraceful end—
He rolled his eye with stern regard

Upon the gentle minstrel bard,
And said in tones abrupt, austere—
'Why, Bracy! dost thou loiter here?
I bade thee hence!' The bard obeyed;
And turning from his own sweet maid,
The agéd knight, Sir Leoline,
Led forth the lady Geraldine!

THE CONCLUSION TO PART II

A little child, a limber elf,
Singing, dancing to itself,
A fairy thing with red round cheeks,
That always finds, and never seeks,
Makes such a vision to the sight
As fills a father's eyes with light;
And pleasures flow in so thick and fast
Upon his heart, that he at last
Must needs express his love's excess
With words of unmeant bitterness.
Perhaps 'tis pretty to force together
Thoughts so all unlike each other;
To mutter and mock a broken charm,
To dally with wrong that does no harm.
Perhaps 'tis tender too and pretty
At each wild word to feel within
A sweet recoil of love and pity.
And what, if in a world of sin
(O sorrow and shame should this be true!)
Such giddiness of heart and brain
Comes seldom save from rage and pain,
So talks as it's most used to do.

Frost at Midnight

The Frost performs its secret ministry,
Unhelped by any wind. The owlet's cry
Came loud—and hark, again! loud as before.
The inmates of my cottage, all at rest,
Have left me to that solitude, which suits
Abstruser musings: save that at my side
My cradled infant slumbers peacefully.
'Tis calm indeed! so calm, that it disturbs
And vexes meditation with its strange
And extreme silentness. Sea, hill, and wood,
This populous village! Sea, and hill, and wood,
With all the numberless goings-on of life,
Inaudible as dreams! the thin blue flame
Lies on my low-burnt fire, and quivers not;
Only that film, which fluttered on the grate,
Still flutters there, the sole unquiet thing.
Methinks, its motion in this hush of nature
Gives it dim sympathies with me who live,
Making it a companionable form,
Whose puny flaps and freaks the idling Spirit
By its own moods interprets, every where
Echo or mirror seeking of itself,
And makes a toy of Thought.

　　　　　　　　　　　But O! how oft,
How oft, at school, with most believing mind,
Presageful, have I gazed upon the bars,
To watch that fluttering *stranger*! and as oft
With unclosed lids, already had I dreamt
Of my sweet birth-place, and the old church-tower,
Whose bells, the poor man's only music, rang
From morn to evening, all the hot Fair-day,
So sweetly, that they stirred and haunted me
With a wild pleasure, falling on mine ear
Most like articulate sounds of things to come!
So gazed I, till the soothing things, I dreamt,
Lulled me to sleep, and sleep prolonged my dreams!

And so I brooded all the following morn,
Awed by the stern preceptor's face, mine eye
Fixed with mock study on my swimming book:
Save if the door half opened, and I snatched
A hasty glance, and still my heart leaped up,
For still I hoped to see the *stranger's* face,
Townsman, or aunt, or sister more beloved,
My play-mate when we both were clothed alike!

   Dear Babe, that sleepest cradled by my side,
Whose gentle breathings, heard in this deep calm,
Fill up the intersperséd vacancies
And momentary pauses of the thought!
My babe so beautiful! it thrills my heart
With tender gladness, thus to look at thee,
And think that thou shalt learn far other lore,
And in far other scenes! For I was reared
In the great city, pent 'mid cloisters dim,
And saw nought lovely but the sky and stars.
But *thou*, my babe! shalt wander like a breeze
By lakes and sandy shores, beneath the crags
Of ancient mountain, and beneath the clouds,
Which image in their bulk both lakes and shores
And mountain crags: so shalt thou see and hear
The lovely shapes and sounds intelligible
Of that eternal language, which thy God
Utters, who from eternity doth teach
Himself in all, and all things in himself.
Great universal Teacher! he shall mould
Thy spirit, and by giving make it ask.

   Therefore all seasons shall be sweet to thee,
Whether the summer clothe the general earth
With greenness, or the redbreast sit and sing
Betwixt the tufts of snow on the bare branch
Of mossy apple-tree, while the nigh thatch
Smokes in the sun-thaw; whether the eave-drops fall
Heard only in the trances of the blast,
Or if the secret ministry of frost
Shall hang them up in silent icicles,
Quietly shining to the quiet Moon.

France: An Ode

I

Ye Clouds! that far above me float and pause,
   Whose pathless march no mortal may controul!
   Ye Ocean-Waves! that, wheresoe'er ye roll,
Yield homage only to eternal laws!
Ye Woods! that listen to the night-birds singing,
   Midway the smooth and perilous slope reclined,
Save when your own imperious branches swinging,
   Have made a solemn music of the wind!
Where, like a man beloved of God,
Through glooms, which never woodman trod,
     How oft, pursuing fancies holy,
My moonlight way o'er flowering weeds I wound,
     Inspired, beyond the guess of folly,
By each rude shape and wild unconquerable sound!
O ye loud Waves! and O ye Forests high!
   And O ye Clouds that far above me soared!
Thou rising Sun! thou blue rejoicing Sky!
   Yea, every thing that is and will be free!
   Bear witness for me, wheresoe'er ye be,
   With what deep worship I have still adored
     The spirit of divinest Liberty.

II

When France in wrath her giant-limbs upreared,
   And with that oath, which smote air, earth, and sea,
   Stamped her strong foot and said she would be free,
Bear witness for me, how I hoped and feared!
With what a joy my lofty gratulation
   Unawed I sang, amid a slavish band:
And when to whelm the disenchanted nation,
   Like fiends embattled by a wizard's wand,
     The Monarchs marched in evil day,
     And Britain joined the dire array;
   Though dear her shores and circling ocean,
Though many friendships, many youthful loves

Had swoln the patriot emotion
And flung a magic light o'er all her hills and groves;
Yet still my voice, unaltered, sang defeat
   To all that braved the tyrant-quelling lance,
And shame too long delayed and vain retreat!
For ne'er, O Liberty! with partial aim
I dimmed thy light or damped thy holy flame;
   But blessed the paeans of delivered France,
And hung my head and wept at Britain's name.

III

'And what,' I said, 'though Blasphemy's loud scream
   With that sweet music of deliverance strove!
   Though all the fierce and drunken passions wove
A dance more wild than e'er was maniac's dream!
   Ye storms, that round the dawning East assembled,
The Sun was rising, though ye hid his light!'
   And when, to soothe my soul, that hoped and trembled,
The dissonance ceased, and all seemed calm and bright;
   When France her front deep-scarr'd and gory
   Concealed with clustering wreaths of glory;
     When, insupportably advancing,
   Her arm made mockery of the warrior's ramp;
     While timid looks of fury glancing,
   Domestic treason, crushed beneath her fatal stamp,
Writhed like a wounded dragon in his gore;
   Then I reproached my fears that would not flee;
'And soon,' I said, 'shall Wisdom teach her lore
In the low huts of them that toil and groan!
And, conquering by her happiness alone,
   Shall France compel the nations to be free,
Till Love and Joy look round, and call the Earth their own.'

IV

Forgive me, Freedom! O forgive those dreams!
   I hear thy voice, I hear thy loud lament,
   From bleak Helvetia's icy caverns sent—
I hear thy groans upon her blood-stained streams!
   Heroes, that for your peaceful country perished,
And ye that, fleeing, spot your mountain-snows

With bleeding wounds; forgive me, that I cherished
One thought that ever blessed your cruel foes!
   To scatter rage, and traitorous guilt,
   Where Peace her jealous home had built;
     A patriot-race to disinherit
Of all that made their stormy wilds so dear;
     And with inexpiable spirit
To taint the bloodless freedom of the mountaineer—
O France, that mockest Heaven, adulterous, blind,
   And patriot only in pernicious toils!
Are these thy boasts, Champion of human kind?
   To mix with Kings in the low lust of sway,
Yell in the hunt, and share the murderous prey;
To insult the shrine of Liberty with spoils
   From freemen torn; to tempt and to betray?

V

   The Sensual and the Dark rebel in vain,
   Slaves by their own compulsion! In mad game
   They burst their manacles and wear the name
     Of Freedom, graven on a heavier chain!
   O Liberty! with profitless endeavour
Have I pursued thee, many a weary hour;
   But thou nor swell'st the victor's strain, nor ever
Didst breathe thy soul in forms of human power.
   Alike from all, howe'er they praise thee,
   (Nor prayer, nor boastful name delays thee)
     Alike from Priestcraft's harpy minions,
   And factious Blasphemy's obscener slaves,
     Thou speedest on thy subtle pinions,
The guide of homeless winds, and playmate of the waves!
And there I felt thee!—on that sea-cliff's verge,
   Whose pines, scarce travelled by the breeze above,
Had made one murmur with the distant surge!
Yes, while I stood and gazed, my temples bare,
And shot my being through earth, sea, and air,
   Possessing all things with intensest love,
     O Liberty! my spirit felt thee there.

Lewti

OR THE CIRCASSIAN LOVE-CHAUNT

At midnight by the stream I roved,
To forget the form I loved.
Image of Lewti! from my mind
Depart; for Lewti is not kind.
The Moon was high, the moonlight gleam
    And the shadow of a star
Heaved upon Tamaha's stream;
    But the rock shone brighter far,
The rock half sheltered from my view
By pendent boughs of tressy yew.—
So shines my Lewti's forehead fair,
Gleaming through her sable hair.
Image of Lewti! from my mind
Depart; for Lewti is not kind.

I saw a cloud of palest hue,
    Onward to the moon it passed;
Still brighter and more bright it grew,
With floating colours not a few,
    Till it reached the moon at last:
Then the cloud was wholly bright,
With a rich and amber light!
And so with many a hope I seek,
    And with such joy I find my Lewti;
And even so my pale wan cheek
    Drinks in as deep a flush of beauty!
Nay, treacherous image! leave my mind,
If Lewti never will be kind.

The little cloud—it floats away,
    Away it goes; away so soon!
Alas! it has no power to stay:
Its hues are dim, its hues are grey—
    Away it passes from the moon!
How mournfully it seems to fly,
    Ever fading more and more,
To joyless regions of the sky—

And now 'tis whiter than before!
As white as my poor cheek will be,
   When, Lewti! on my couch I lie,
A dying man for love of thee.
Nay, treacherous image! leave my mind—
And yet, thou didst not look unkind.

I saw a vapour in the sky,
Thin, and white, and very high;
I ne'er beheld so thin a cloud:
   Perhaps the breezes that can fly
   Now below and now above,
Have snatched aloft the lawny shroud
   Of Lady fair—that died for love.
For maids, as well as youths, have perished
From fruitless love too fondly cherished.
Nay, treacherous image! leave my mind—
For Lewti never will be kind.

Hush! my heedless feet from under
   Slip the crumbling banks for ever:
Like echoes to a distant thunder,
   They plunge into the gentle river.
The river-swans have heard my tread,
And startle from their reedy bed.
O beauteous birds! methinks ye measure
   Your movements to some heavenly tune!
O beauteous birds! 'tis such a pleasure
   To see you move beneath the moon,
I would it were your true delight
To sleep by day and wake all night.

I know the place where Lewti lies,
When silent night has closed her eyes:
   It is a breezy jasmine-bower,
The nightingale sings o'er her head:
   Voice of the Night! had I the power
That leafy labyrinth to thread,
And creep, like thee, with soundless tread,
I then might view her bosom white
Heaving lovely to my sight,

As these two swans together heave
On the gently-swelling wave.

Oh! that she saw me in a dream,
    And dreamt that I had died for care;
All pale and wasted I would seem,
    Yet fair withal, as spirits are!
I'd die indeed, if I might see
Her bosom heave, and heave for me!
Soothe, gentle image! soothe my mind!
To-morrow Lewti may be kind.

Fears in Solitude

WRITTEN IN APRIL 1798, DURING THE
ALARM OF AN INVASION

A green and silent spot, amid the hills,
A small and silent dell! O'er stiller place
No singing sky-lark ever poised himself.
The hills are heathy, save that swelling slope,
Which hath a gay and gorgeous covering on,
All golden with the never-bloomless furze,
Which now blooms most profusely: but the dell,
Bathed by the mist, is fresh and delicate
As vernal corn-field, or the unripe flax,
When, through its half-transparent stalks, at eve,
The level sunshine glimmers with green light.
Oh! 'tis a quiet spirit-healing nook!
Which all, methinks, would love; but chiefly he,
The humble man, who, in his youthful years,
Knew just so much of folly, as had made
His early manhood more securely wise!
Here he might lie on fern or withered heath,
While from the singing lark (that sings unseen
The minstrelsy that solitude loves best),
And from the sun, and from the breezy air,
Sweet influences trembled o'er his frame;
And he, with many feelings, many thoughts,
Made up a meditative joy, and found

Religious meanings in the forms of Nature!
And so, his senses gradually wrapt
In a half sleep, he dreams of better worlds,
And dreaming hears thee still, O singing lark,
That singest like an angel in the clouds!

My God! it is a melancholy thing
For such a man, who would full fain preserve
His soul in calmness, yet perforce must feel
For all his human brethren—O my God!
It weighs upon the heart, that he must think
What uproar and what strife may now be stirring
This way or that way o'er these silent hills—
Invasion, and the thunder and the shout,
And all the crash of onset; fear and rage,
And undetermined conflict—even now,
Even now, perchance, and in his native isle:
Carnage and groans beneath this blessed sun!
We have offended, Oh! my countrymen!
We have offended very grievously,
And been most tyrannous. From east to west
A groan of accusation pierces Heaven!
The wretched plead against us; multitudes
Countless and vehement, the sons of God,
Our brethren! Like a cloud that travels on,
Steamed up from Cairo's swamps of pestilence,
Even so, my countrymen! have we gone forth
And borne to distant tribes slavery and pangs,
And, deadlier far, our vices, whose deep taint
With slow perdition murders the whole man,
His body and his soul! Meanwhile, at home,
All individual dignity and power
Engulfed in Courts, Committees, Institutions,
Associations and Societies,
A vain, speech-mouthing, speech-reporting Guild,
One Benefit-Club for mutual flattery,
We have drunk up, demure as at a grace,
Pollutions from the brimming cup of wealth;
Contemptuous of all honourable rule,
Yet bartering freedom and the poor man's life
For gold, as at a market! The sweet words

Of Christian promise, words that even yet
Might stem destruction, were they wisely preached,
Are muttered o'er by men, whose tones proclaim
How flat and wearisome they feel their trade:
Rank scoffers some, but most too indolent
To deem them falsehoods or to know their truth.
Oh! blasphemous! the Book of Life is made
A superstitious instrument, on which
We gabble o'er the oaths we mean to break;
For all must swear—all and in every place,
College and wharf, council and justice-court;
All, all must swear, the briber and the bribed,
Merchant and lawyer, senator and priest,
The rich, the poor, the old man and the young;
All, all make up one scheme of perjury,
That faith doth reel; the very name of God
Sounds like a juggler's charm; and, bold with joy,
Forth from his dark and lonely hiding-place,
(Portentous sight!) the owlet Atheism,
Sailing on obscene wings athwart the noon,
Drops his blue-fringéd lids, and holds them close,
And hooting at the glorious sun in Heaven,
Cries out, 'Where is it?'

        Thankless too for peace,
(Peace long preserved by fleets and perilous seas)
Secure from actual warfare, we have loved
To swell the war-whoop, passionate for war!
Alas! for ages ignorant of all
Its ghastlier workings, (famine or blue plague,
Battle, or siege, or flight through wintry snows,)
We, this whole people, have been clamorous
For war and bloodshed; animating sports,
The which we pay for as a thing to talk of,
Spectators and not combatants! No guess
Anticipative of a wrong unfelt,
No speculation on contingency,
However dim and vague, too vague and dim
To yield a justifying cause; and forth,
(Stuffed out with big preamble, holy names,
And adjurations of the God in Heaven,)

We send our mandates for the certain death
Of thousands and ten thousands! Boys and girls,
And women, that would groan to see a child
Pull off an insect's leg, all read of war,
The best amusement for our morning meal!
The poor wretch, who has learnt his only prayers
From curses, who knows scarcely words enough
To ask a blessing from his Heavenly Father,
Becomes a fluent phraseman, absolute
And technical in victories and defeats,
And all our dainty terms for fratricide;
Terms which we trundle smoothly o'er our tongues
Like mere abstractions, empty sounds to which
We join no feeling and attach no form!
As if the soldier died without a wound;
As if the fibres of this godlike frame
Were gored without a pang; as if the wretch,
Who fell in battle, doing bloody deeds,
Passed off to Heaven, translated and not killed;
As though he had no wife to pine for him,
No God to judge him! Therefore, evil days
Are coming on us, O my countrymen!
And what if all-avenging Providence,
Strong and retributive, should make us know
The meaning of our words, force us to feel
The desolation and the agony
Of our fierce doings?

        Spare us yet awhile,
Father and God! O! spare us yet awhile!
Oh! let not English women drag their flight
Fainting beneath the burthen of their babes,
Of the sweet infants, that but yesterday
Laughed at the breast! Sons, brothers, husbands, all
Who ever gazed with fondness on the forms
Which grew up with you round the same fire-side,
And all who ever heard the sabbath-bells
Without the infidel's scorn, make yourselves pure!
Stand forth! be men! repel an impious foe,
Impious and false, a light yet cruel race,
Who laugh away all virtue, mingling mirth
With deeds of murder; and still promising

Freedom, themselves too sensual to be free,
Poison life's amities, and cheat the heart
Of faith and quiet hope, and all that soothes,
And all that lifts the spirit! Stand we forth;
Render them back upon the insulted ocean,
And let them toss as idly on its waves
As the vile sea-weed, which some mountain-blast
Swept from our shores! And oh! may we return
Not with a drunken triumph, but with fear,
Repenting of the wrongs with which we stung
So fierce a foe to frenzy!

                  I have told,
O Britons! O my brethren! I have told
Most bitter truth, but without bitterness.
Nor deem my zeal or factious or mistimed;
For never can true courage dwell with them,
Who, playing tricks with conscience, dare not look
At their own vices. We have been too long
Dupes of a deep delusion! Some, belike,
Groaning with restless enmity, expect
All change from change of constituted power;
As if a Government had been a robe,
On which our vice and wretchedness were tagged
Like fancy-points and fringes, with the robe
Pulled off at pleasure. Fondly these attach
A radical causation to a few
Poor drudges of chastising Providence,
Who borrow all their hues and qualities
From our own folly and rank wickedness,
Which gave them birth and nursed them. Others,
      meanwhile,
Dote with a mad idolatry; and all
Who will not fall before their images,
And yield them worship, they are enemies
Even of their country!

                Such have I been deemed.—
But, O dear Britain! O my Mother Isle!
Needs must thou prove a name most dear and holy
To me, a son, a brother, and a friend,
A husband, and a father! who revere

All bonds of natural love, and find them all
Within the limits of thy rocky shores.
O native Britain! O my Mother Isle!
How shouldst thou prove aught else but dear and holy
To me, who from thy lakes and mountain-hills,
Thy clouds, thy quiet dales, thy rocks and seas,
Have drunk in all my intellectual life,
All sweet sensations, all ennobling thoughts,
All adoration of the God in nature,
All lovely and all honourable things,
Whatever makes this mortal spirit feel
The joy and greatness of its future being?
There lives nor form nor feeling in my soul
Unborrowed from my country! O divine
And beauteous island! thou hast been my sole
And most magnificent temple, in the which
I walk with awe, and sing my stately songs,
Loving the God that made me!—

                                        May my fears,
My filial fears, be vain! and may the vaunts
And menace of the vengeful enemy
Pass like the gust, that roared and died away
In the distant tree: which heard, and only heard
In this low dell, bowed not the delicate grass.

    But now the gentle dew-fall sends abroad
The fruit-like perfume of the golden furze:
The light has left the summit of the hill,
Though still a sunny gleam lies beautiful,
Aslant the ivied beacon. Now farewell,
Farewell, awhile, O soft and silent spot!
On the green sheep-track, up the heathy hill,
Homeward I wind my way; and lo! recalled
From bodings that have well-nigh wearied me,
I find myself upon the brow, and pause
Startled! And after lonely sojourning
In such a quiet and surrounded nook,
This burst of prospect, here the shadowy main,
Dim-tinted, there the mighty majesty
Of that huge amphitheatre of rich
And elmy fields, seems like society—

Conversing with the mind, and giving it
A livelier impulse and a dance of thought!
And now, belovéd Stowey! I behold
Thy church-tower, and, methinks, the four huge elms
Clustering, which mark the mansion of my friend;
And close behind them, hidden from my view,
Is my own lowly cottage, where my babe
And my babe's mother dwell in peace! With light
And quickened footsteps thitherward I tend,
Remembering thee, O green and silent dell!
And grateful, that by nature's quietness
And solitary musings, all my heart
Is softened, and made worthy to indulge
Love, and the thoughts that yearn for human kind.

The Nightingale

A CONVERSATION POEM, APRIL, 1798

No cloud, no relique of the sunken day
Distinguishes the West, no long thin slip
Of sullen light, no obscure trembling hues.
Come, we will rest on this old mossy bridge!
You see the glimmer of the stream beneath,
But hear no murmuring: it flows silently,
O'er its soft bed of verdure. All is still,
A balmy night! and though the stars be dim,
Yet let us think upon the vernal showers
That gladden the green earth, and we shall find
A pleasure in the dimness of the stars.
And hark! the Nightingale begins its song,
'Most musical, most melancholy' bird!
A melancholy bird? Oh! idle thought!
In Nature there is nothing melancholy.
But some night-wandering man whose heart was pierced
With the remembrance of a grievous wrong,
Or slow distemper, or neglected love,
(And so, poor wretch! filled all things with himself,
And made all gentle sounds tell back the tale
Of his own sorrow) he, and such as he,

First named these notes a melancholy strain.
And many a poet echoes the conceit;
Poet who hath been building up the rhyme
When he had better far have stretched his limbs
Beside a brook in mossy forest-dell,
By sun or moon-light, to the influxes
Of shapes and sounds and shifting elements
Surrendering his whole spirit, of his song
And of his fame forgetful! so his fame
Should share in Nature's immortality,
A venerable thing! and so his song
Should make all Nature lovelier, and itself
Be loved like Nature! But 'twill not be so;
And youths and maidens most poetical,
Who lose the deepening twilights of the spring
In ball-rooms and hot theatres, they still
Full of meek sympathy must heave their sighs
O'er Philomela's pity-pleading strains.

My Friend, and thou, our Sister! we have learnt
A different lore: we may not thus profane
Nature's sweet voices, always full of love
And joyance! 'Tis the merry Nightingale
That crowds, and hurries, and precipitates
With fast thick warble his delicious notes,
As he were fearful that an April night
Would be too short for him to utter forth
His love-chant, and disburthen his full soul
Of all its music!
                    And I know a grove
Of large extent, hard by a castle huge,
Which the great lord inhabits not; and so
This grove is wild with tangling underwood,
And the trim walks are broken up, and grass,
Thin grass and king-cups grow within the paths.
But never elsewhere in one place I knew
So many nightingales; and far and near,
In wood and thicket, over the wide grove,
They answer and provoke each other's song,
With skirmish and capricious passagings,
And murmurs musical and swift jug jug,

And one low piping sound more sweet than all—
Stirring the air with such a harmony,
That should you close your eyes, you might almost
Forget it was not day! On moonlight bushes,
Whose dewy leaflets are but half-disclosed,
You may perchance behold them on the twigs,
Their bright, bright eyes, their eyes both bright and full,
Glistening, while many a glow-worm in the shade
Lights up her love-torch.
                                  A most gentle Maid,
Who dwelleth in her hospitable home
Hard by the castle, and at latest eve
(Even like a Lady vowed and dedicate
To something more than Nature in the grove)
Glides through the pathways; she knows all their notes,
That gentle Maid! and oft, a moment's space,
What time the moon was lost behind a cloud,
Hath heard a pause of silence; till the moon
Emerging, hath awakened earth and sky
With one sensation, and those wakeful birds
Have all burst forth in choral minstrelsy,
As if some sudden gale had swept at once
A hundred airy harps! And she hath watched
Many a nightingale perch giddily
On blossomy twig still swinging from the breeze,
And to that motion tune his wanton song
Like tipsy Joy that reels with tossing head.

Farewell, O Warbler! till to-morrow eve,
And you, my friends! farewell, a short farewell!
We have been loitering long and pleasantly,
And now for our dear homes.—That strain again!
Full fain it would delay me! My dear babe,
Who, capable of no articulate sound,
Mars all things with his imitative lisp,
How he would place his hand beside his ear,
His little hand, the small forefinger up,
And bid us listen! And I deem it wise
To make him Nature's play-mate. He knows well
The evening-star; and once, when he awoke
In most distressful mood (some inward pain

Had made up that strange thing, an infant's dream—)
I hurried with him to our orchard-plot,
And he beheld the moon, and, hushed at once,
Suspends his sobs, and laughs most silently,
While his fair eyes, that swam with undropped tears,
Did glitter in the yellow moon-beam! Well!—
It is a father's tale: But if that Heaven
Should give me life, his childhood shall grow up
Familiar with these songs, that with the night
He may associate joy.—Once more, farewell,
Sweet Nightingale! once more, my friends! farewell.

Kubla Khan

In Xanadu did Kubla Khan
A stately pleasure-dome decree:
Where Alph, the sacred river, ran
Through caverns measureless to man
    Down to a sunless sea.
So twice five miles of fertile ground
With walls and towers were girdled round:
And there were gardens bright with sinuous rills,
Where blossomed many an incense-bearing tree;
And here were forests ancient as the hills,
Enfolding sunny spots of greenery.

But oh! that deep romantic chasm which slanted
Down the green hill athwart a cedarn cover!
A savage place! as holy and enchanted
As e'er beneath a waning moon was haunted
By woman wailing for her demon-lover!
And from this chasm, with ceaseless turmoil seething,
As if this earth in fast thick pants were breathing,
A mighty fountain momently was forced:
Amid whose swift half-intermitted burst
Huge fragments vaulted like rebounding hail,
Or chaffy grain beneath the thresher's flail:
And 'mid these dancing rocks at once and ever

It flung up momently the sacred river.
Five miles meandering with a mazy motion
Through wood and dale the sacred river ran,
Then reached the caverns measureless to man,
And sank in tumult to a lifeless ocean:
And 'mid this tumult Kubla heard from far
Ancestral voices prophesying war!
   The shadow of the dome of pleasure
   Floated midway on the waves;
   Where was heard the mingled measure
   From the fountain and the caves.
It was a miracle of rare device,
A sunny pleasure-dome with caves of ice!

   A damsel with a dulcimer
   In a vision once I saw:
   It was an Abyssinian maid,
   And on her dulcimer she played,
   Singing of Mount Abora.
   Could I revive within me
   Her symphony and song,
   To such a deep delight 'twould win me,
That with music loud and long,
I would build that dome in air,
That sunny dome! those caves of ice!
And all who heard should see them there,
And all should cry, Beware! Beware!
His flashing eyes, his floating hair!
Weave a circle round him thrice,
And close your eyes with holy dread,
For he on honey-dew hath fed,
And drunk the milk of Paradise.

The Ovidian Elegiac Metre

DESCRIBED AND EXEMPLIFIED

In the hexameter rises the fountain's silvery column;
In the pentameter aye falling in melody back.

Something Childish, but Very Natural

WRITTEN IN GERMANY

If I had but two little wings
    And were a little feathery bird,
        To you I'd fly, my dear!
But thoughts like these are idle things,
        And I stay here.

But in my sleep to you I fly:
    I'm always with you in my sleep!
        The world is all one's own.
But then one wakes, and where am I?
        All, all alone.

Sleep stays not, though a monarch bids:
    So I love to wake ere break of day:
        For though my sleep be gone,
Yet while 'tis dark, one shuts one's lids,
        And still dreams on.

Love

All thoughts, all passions, all delights,
Whatever stirs this mortal frame,
All are but ministers of Love,
        And feed his sacred flame.

Oft in my waking dreams do I
Live o'er again that happy hour,
When midway on the mount I lay,
        Beside the ruined tower.

The moonshine, stealing o'er the scene
Had blended with the lights of eve;
And she was there, my hope, my joy,
        My own dear Genevieve!

She leant against the arméd man,
The statue of the arméd knight;
She stood and listened to my lay,
  Amid the lingering light.

Few sorrows hath she of her own,
My hope! my joy! my Genevieve!
She loves me best, whene'er I sing
  The songs that make her grieve.

I played a soft and doleful air,
I sang an old and moving story—
An old rude song, that suited well
  That ruin wild and hoary.

She listened with a flitting blush,
With downcast eyes and modest grace;
For well she knew, I could not choose
  But gaze upon her face.

I told her of the Knight that wore
Upon his shield a burning brand;
And that for ten long years he wooed
  The Lady of the Land.

I told her how he pined: and ah!
The deep, the low, the pleading tone
With which I sang another's love,
  Interpreted my own.

She listened with a flitting blush,
With downcast eyes, and modest grace;
And she forgave me, that I gazed
  Too fondly on her face!

But when I told the cruel scorn
That crazed that bold and lovely Knight,
And that he crossed the mountain-woods,
  Nor rested day nor night;

That sometimes from the savage den,
And sometimes from the darksome shade,
And sometimes starting up at once
  In green and sunny glade,—

There came and looked him in the face
An angel beautiful and bright;
And that he knew it was a Fiend,
    This miserable Knight!

And that unknowing what he did,
He leaped amid a murderous band,
And saved from outrage worse than death
    The Lady of the Land!

And how she wept, and clasped his knees;
And how she tended him in vain—
And ever strove to expiate
    The scorn that crazed his brain;—

And that she nursed him in a cave;
And how his madness went away,
When on the yellow forest-leaves
    A dying man he lay;—

His dying words—but when I reached
That tenderest strain of all the ditty,
My faultering voice and pausing harp
    Disturbed her soul with pity!

All impulses of soul and sense
Had thrilled my guileless Genevieve;
The music and the doleful tale,
    The rich and balmy eve;

And hopes, and fears that kindle hope,
An undistinguishable throng,
And gentle wishes long subdued,
    Subdued and cherished long!

She wept with pity and delight,
She blushed with love, and virgin-shame;
And like the murmur of a dream,
    I heard her breathe my name.

Her bosom heaved—she stepped aside,
As conscious of my look she stepped—
Then suddenly, with timorous eye
    She fled to me and wept.

She half enclosed me with her arms,
She pressed me with a meek embrace;
And bending back her head, looked up,
      And gazed upon my face.

'Twas partly love, and partly fear,
And partly 'twas a bashful art,
That I might rather feel, than see,
      The swelling of her heart.

I calmed her fears, and she was calm,
And told her love with virgin pride;
And so I won my Genevieve,
      My bright and beauteous Bride.

Dejection: An Ode

Late, late yestreen I saw the new Moon,
With the old Moon in her arms;
And I fear, I fear, my Master dear!
We shall have a deadly storm.
            Ballad of Sir Patrick Spence.

I

Well! If the Bard was weather-wise, who made
   The grand old ballad of Sir Patrick Spence,
   This night, so tranquil now, will not go hence
Unroused by winds, that ply a busier trade
Than those which mould yon cloud in lazy flakes,
Or the dull sobbing draft, that moans and rakes
Upon the strings of this Æolian lute,
      Which better far were mute.
   For lo! the New-moon winter-bright!
   And overspread with phantom light,
   (With swimming phantom light o'erspread
   But rimmed and circled by a silver thread)
I see the old Moon in her lap, foretelling
   The coming-on of rain and squally blast.

And oh! that even now the gust were swelling,
   And the slant night-shower driving loud and fast!
Those sounds which oft have raised me, whilst they awed,
     And sent my soul abroad,
Might now perhaps their wonted impulse give,
Might startle this dull pain, and make it move and live!

II

A grief without a pang, void, dark, and drear,
   A stifled, drowsy, unimpassioned grief,
   Which finds no natural outlet, no relief,
     In word, or sigh, or tear—
O Lady! in this wan and heartless mood,
To other thoughts by yonder throstle woo'd,
  All this long eve, so balmy and serene,
Have I been gazing on the western sky,
  And its peculiar tint of yellow green:
And still I gaze—and with how blank an eye!
And those thin clouds above, in flakes and bars,
That give away their motion to the stars;
Those stars, that glide behind them or between,
Now sparkling, now bedimmed, but always seen:
Yon crescent Moon, as fixed as if it grew
In its own cloudless, starless lake of blue;
I see them all so excellently fair,
I see, not feel, how beautiful they are!

III

   My genial spirits fail;
   And what can these avail
To lift the smothering weight from off my breast?
   It were a vain endeavour,
   Though I should gaze for ever
On that green light that lingers in the west:
I may not hope from outward forms to win
The passion and the life, whose fountains are within.

IV

O Lady! we receive but what we give,
And in our life alone does Nature live:

Ours is her wedding garment, ours her shroud!
   And would we aught behold, of higher worth,
Than that inanimate cold world allowed
To the poor loveless ever-anxious crowd,
   Ah! from the soul itself must issue forth
A light, a glory, a fair luminous cloud
      Enveloping the Earth—
And from the soul itself must there be sent
   A sweet and potent voice, of its own birth,
Of all sweet sounds the life and element!

V

O pure of heart! thou need'st not ask of me
What this strong music in the soul may be!
What, and wherein it doth exist,
This light, this glory, this fair luminous mist,
This beautiful and beauty-making power.
   Joy, virtuous Lady! Joy that ne'er was given,
Save to the pure, and in their purest hour,
Life, and Life's effluence, cloud at once and shower,
Joy, Lady! is the spirit and the power,
Which wedding Nature to us gives in dower
   A new Earth and new Heaven,
Undreamt of by the sensual and the proud—
Joy is the sweet voice, Joy the luminous cloud—
      We in ourselves rejoice!
And thence flows all that charms or ear or sight,
   All melodies the echoes of that voice,
All colours a suffusion from that light.

VI

There was a time when, though my path was rough,
   This joy within me dallied with distress,
And all misfortunes were but as the stuff
   Whence Fancy made me dreams of happiness:
For hope grew round me, like the twining vine,
And fruits, and foliage, not my own, seemed mine.
But now afflictions bow me down to earth:
Nor care I that they rob me of my mirth;
      But oh! each visitation

Suspends what nature gave me at my birth,
   My shaping spirit of Imagination.
For not to think of what I needs must feel,
   But to be still and patient, all I can;
And haply by abstruse research to steal
   From my own nature all the natural man—
   This was my sole resource, my only plan:
Till that which suits a part infects the whole,
And now is almost grown the habit of my soul.

VII

Hence, viper thoughts, that coil around my mind,
    Reality's dark dream!
I turn from you, and listen to the wind,
   Which long has raved unnoticed. What a scream
Of agony by torture lengthened out
That lute sent forth! Thou Wind, that rav'st without,
   Bare crag, or mountain-tairn, or blasted tree,
Or pine-grove whither woodman never clomb,
Or lonely house, long held the witches' home,
   Methinks were fitter instruments for thee,
Mad Lutanist! who in this month of showers,
Of dark-brown gardens, and of peeping flowers,
Mak'st Devils' yule, with worse than wintry song,
The blossoms, buds, and timorous leaves among.
   Thou Actor, perfect in all tragic sounds!
Thou mighty Poet, e'en to frenzy bold!
    What tell'st thou now about?
    'Tis of the rushing of an host in rout,
   With groans, of trampled men, with smarting wounds—
At once they groan with pain, and shudder with the cold!
But hush! there is a pause of deepest silence!
   And all that noise, as of a rushing crowd,
With groans, and tremulous shudderings—all is over—
   It tells another tale, with sounds less deep and loud!
    A tale of less affright,
    And tempered with delight,
As Otway's self had framed the tender lay,—
    'Tis of a little child
    Upon a lonesome wild,

Not far from home, but she hath lost her way:
And now moans low in bitter grief and fear,
And now screams loud, and hopes to make her mother hear.

VIII

'Tis midnight, but small thoughts have I of sleep:
Full seldom may my friend such vigils keep!
Visit her, gentle Sleep! with wings of healing,
    And may this storm be but a mountain-birth,
May all the stars hang bright above her dwelling,
    Silent as though they watched the sleeping Earth!
        With light heart may she rise,
        Gay fancy, cheerful eyes,
    Joy lift her spirit, joy attune her voice;
To her may all things live, from pole to pole,
Their life the eddying of her living soul!
    O simple spirit, guided from above,
Dear Lady! friend devoutest of my choice,
Thus mayest thou ever, evermore rejoice.

The Pains of Sleep

Ere on my bed my limbs I lay,
It hath not been my use to pray
With moving lips or bended knees;
But silently, by slow degrees,
My spirit I to Love compose,
In humble trust mine eye-lids close,
With reverential resignation,
No wish conceived, no thought exprest,
Only a sense of supplication;
A sense o'er all my soul imprest
That I am weak, yet not unblest,
Since in me, round me, every where
Eternal Strength and Wisdom are.

But yester-night I prayed aloud
In anguish and in agony,

Up-starting from the fiendish crowd
Of shapes and thoughts that tortured me:
A lurid light, a trampling throng,
Sense of intolerable wrong,
And whom I scorned, those only strong!
Thirst of revenge, the powerless will
Still baffled, and yet burning still!
Desire with loathing strangely mixed
On wild or hateful objects fixed.
Fantastic passions! maddening brawl!
And shame and terror over all!
Deeds to be hid which were not hid,
Which all confused I could not know
Whether I suffered, or I did:
For all seemed guilt, remorse or woe,
My own or others still the same
Life-stifling fear, soul-stifling shame.

So two nights passed: the night's dismay
Saddened and stunned the coming day.
Sleep, the wide blessing, seemed to me
Distemper's worst calamity.
The third night, when my own loud scream
Had waked me from the fiendish dream,
O'ercome with sufferings strange and wild,
I wept as I had been a child;
And having thus by tears subdued
My anguish to a milder mood,
Such punishments, I said, were due
To natures deepliest stained with sin,—
For aye entempesting anew
The unfathomable hell within,
The horror of their deeds to view,
To know and loathe, yet wish and do!
Such griefs with such men well agree,
But wherefore, wherefore fall on me?
To be beloved is all I need,
And whom I love, I love indeed.

To William Wordsworth

COMPOSED ON THE NIGHT AFTER HIS
RECITATION OF A POEM ON THE GROWTH
OF AN INDIVIDUAL MIND

Friend of the wise! and Teacher of the Good!
Into my heart have I received that Lay
More than historic, that prophetic Lay
Wherein (high theme by thee first sung aright)
Of the foundations and the building up
Of a Human Spirit thou hast dared to tell
What may be told, to the understanding mind
Revealable; and what within the mind
By vital breathings secret as the soul
Of vernal growth, oft quickens in the heart
Thoughts all too deep for words!—

                        Theme hard as high!
Of smiles spontaneous, and mysterious fears
(The first-born they of Reason and twin-birth),
Of tides obedient to external force,
And currents self-determined, as might seem,
Or by some inner Power; of moments awful,
Now in thy inner life, and now abroad,
When power streamed from thee, and thy soul received
The light reflected, as a light bestowed—
Of fancies fair, and milder hours of youth,
Hyblean murmurs of poetic thought
Industrious in its joy, in vales and glens
Native or outland, lakes and famous hills!
Or on the lonely high-road, when the stars
Were rising; or by secret mountain-streams,
The guides and the companions of thy way!

Of more than Fancy, of the Social Sense
Distending wide, and man beloved as man,
Where France in all her towns lay vibrating
Like some becalméd bark beneath the burst
Of Heaven's immediate thunder, when no cloud
Is visible, or shadow on the main.

For thou wert there, thine own brows garlanded,
Amid the tremor of a realm aglow,
Amid a mighty nation jubilant,
When from the general heart of human kind
Hope sprang forth like a full-born Deity!
——Of that dear Hope afflicted and struck down,
So summoned homeward, thenceforth calm and sure
From the dread watch-tower of man's absolute self,
With light unwaning on her eyes, to look
Far on—herself a glory to behold,
The Angel of the vision! Then (last strain)
Of Duty, chosen Laws controlling choice,
Action and joy!—An Orphic song indeed,
A song divine of high and passionate thoughts
To their own music chaunted!

                   O great Bard!
Ere yet that last strain dying awed the air,
With stedfast eye I viewed thee in the choir
Of ever-enduring men. The truly great
Have all one age, and from one visible space
Shed influence! They, both in power and act,
Are permanent, and Time is not with them,
Save as it worketh for them, they in it.
Nor less a sacred Roll, than those of old,
And to be placed, as they, with gradual fame
Among the archives of mankind, thy work
Makes audible a linkéd lay of Truth,
Of Truth profound a sweet continuous lay,
Not learnt, but native, her own natural notes!
Ah! as I listened with a heart forlorn,
The pulses of my being beat anew:
And even as Life returns upon the drowned,
Life's joy rekindling roused a throng of pains
Keen pangs of Love, awakening as a babe
Turbulent, with an outcry in the heart;
And fears self-willed, that shunned the eye of Hope;
And Hope that scarce would know itself from Fear;
Sense of past Youth, and Manhood come in vain,
And Genius given, and Knowledge won in vain;
And all which I had culled in wood-walks wild,

And all which patient toil had reared, and all,
Commune with thee had opened out—but flowers
Strewed on my corse, and borne upon my bier
In the same coffin, for the self-same grave!

    That way no more! and ill beseems it me,
Who came a welcomer in herald's guise,
Singing of Glory, and Futurity,
To wander back on such unhealthful road,
Plucking the poisons of self-harm! And ill
Such intertwine beseems triumphal wreaths
Strew'd before thy advancing!

                              Nor do thou,
Sage Bard! impair the memory of that hour
Of thy communion with my nobler mind
By pity or grief, already felt too long!
Nor let my words import more blame than needs.
The tumult rose and ceased: for Peace is nigh
Where Wisdom's voice has found a listening heart.
Amid the howl of more than wintry storms,
The Halcyon hears the voice of vernal hours
Already on the wing.

                    Eve following eve,
Dear tranquil time, when the sweet sense of Home
Is sweetest! moments for their own sake hailed
And more desired, more precious, for thy song,
In silence listening, like a devout child,
My soul lay passive, by thy various strain
Driven as in surges now beneath the stars,
With momentary stars of my own birth,
Fair constellated foam, still darting off
Into the darkness; now a tranquil sea,
Outspread and bright, yet swelling to the moon.

And when—O Friend! my comforter and guide!
Strong in thyself, and powerful to give strength!—
Thy long sustainéd Song finally closed,
And thy deep voice had ceased—yet thou thyself
Wert still before my eyes, and round us both
That happy vision of belovéd faces—
Scarce conscious, and yet conscious of its close

I sate, my being blended in one thought
(Thought was it? or aspiration? or resolve?)
Absorbed, yet hanging still upon the sound—
And when I rose, I found myself in prayer.

The Knight's Tomb

Where is the grave of Sir Arthur O'Kellyn?
Where may the grave of that good man be?—
By the side of a spring, on the breast of Helvellyn,
Under the twigs of a young birch tree!
The oak that in summer was sweet to hear,
And rustled its leaves in the fall of the year,
And whistled and roared in the winter alone,
Is gone,—and the birch in its stead is grown.—
The Knight's bones are dust,
And his good sword rust;—
His soul is with the saints, I trust.

On Donne's Poetry

With Donne, whose muse on dromedary trots,
Wreathe iron pokers into true-love knots;
Rhyme's sturdy cripple, fancy's maze and clue,
Wit's forge and fire-blast, meaning's press and screw.

Youth and Age

Verse, a breeze mid blossoms straying,
Where Hope clung feeding, like a bee—
Both were mine! Life went a-maying
        With Nature, Hope, and Poesy,
                When I was young!

When I was young?—Ah, woful When!
Ah! for the change 'twixt Now and Then!
This breathing house not built with hands,
This body that does me grievous wrong,
O'er aery cliffs and glittering sands,
How lightly then it flashed along:—
Like those trim skiffs, unknown of yore,
On winding lakes and rivers wide,
That ask no aid of sail or oar,
That fear no spite of wind or tide!
Nought cared this body for wind or weather
When Youth and I lived in't together.

Flowers are lovely; Love is flower-like;
Friendship is a sheltering tree;
O! the joys, that came down shower-like,
Of Friendship, Love, and Liberty,
                              Ere I was old!

Ere I was old? Ah woful Ere,
Which tells me, Youth's no longer here!
O Youth! for years so many and sweet,
'Tis known, that Thou and I were one,
I'll think it but a fond conceit—
It cannot be that Thou art gone!
Thy vesper-bell hath not yet toll'd:—
And thou wert aye a masker bold!
What strange disguise hast now put on,
To make believe, that thou art gone?
I see these locks in silvery slips,
This drooping gait, this altered size:
But Spring-tide blossoms on thy lips,
And tears take sunshine from thine eyes!
Life is but thought: so think I will
That Youth and I are house-mates still.

Dew-drops are the gems of morning,
But the tears of mournful eve!
Where no hope is, life's a warning
That only serves to make us grieve,
                              When we are old:

That only serves to make us grieve
With oft and tedious taking-leave,
Like some poor nigh-related guest,
That may not rudely be dismist;
Yet hath outstay'd his welcome while,
And tells the jest without the smile.

Cologne

In Köhln, a town of monks and bones,
And pavements fang'd with murderous stones
And rags, and hags, and hideous wenches;
I counted two and seventy stenches,
All well defined, and several stinks!
Ye Nymphs that reign o'er sewers and sinks,
The river Rhine, it is well known,
Doth wash your city of Cologne;
But tell me, Nymphs, what power divine
Shall henceforth wash the river Rhine?

Alphabetical List of Titles

Alphabetical List of First Lines